TAKE IT TO THE LIMIT

THE STORY OF A SHEFFIELD ROCK'N'ROLL LEGEND

BY NEIL ANDERSON

Published by
ACMRETRO

ISBN: 978-0-9563649-0-6

Every effort has been made to trace the copyright holders of photographers in this book but one or two were unreachable. We would be grateful if the photographers concerned would contact us.

ACMRETRO

Published by ACM Retro, The Grange,
Church Street,
Dronfield,
Sheffield S18 1QB.

Visit ACM Retro at
www.acmretro.com

Published by ACM Retro 2009.

A catalogue record for this book is available from the British Library.

Front cover photos by Pete Hill.
Back cover photos by Bailey Brothers,
Gary Wilson, and Geoffrey Beattie.

Dedicated to
Lowri and Ewan

Photo: Pete Hill

Siouxsie Sioux at The Limit

TAKE IT TO THE LIMIT

CONTENTS

Limit regulars Laura Deeley and Allison Bowen Photo: Tracy Pidd

TAKE IT TO THE LIMIT

THE STORY OF A SHEFFIELD ROCK'N'ROLL LEGEND

It's unlikely that any Sheffield venue will ever leave a legacy quite like that of The Limit. You'd be hard-pressed even to find another one nationally that made such an impact at the time.

The influence of the West Street venue is as strong today as it was the day the place shut in 1991.

"The Limit club was one of the first things I heard about when I arrived in Sheffield,"admits celebrated Sheffield / Berlin-based DJ and promoter Ralph Razor.

Not bad considering the place shut a good decade before he landed in the city.

Manchester has waxed lyrical about its Hacienda for years; it's about time Steel City did the same with The Limit.

At least Sheffield's shrine to excess (mostly lager-charged rather than anything overly illicit) actually made money, unlike its Lancashire counterpart.

It's unlikely anyone will ever know precisely how much cash changed hands over its ticket counter and bars during its 13-year reign but an alternative moniker - 'licence to print money' - was offered by interviewee after interviewee in the writing of this book.

The ease with which The Limit generated vast amounts of cash was significant: it triggered a massive VAT investigation which threatened to close the place permanently; it also funded the rock-star lifestyles of senior management, helped send a few egos out of control and hiked up expensive divorce settlements. It also covered all the other pre-requisites involved in running what was probably the North of England's most successful alternative venue ever.

> "The Limit club was one of the first things I heard about when I arrived in Sheffield."
> Ralph Razor

So where did all the madness begin, the madness that played a hand in the rise of everyone from Human League to U2 in its 13-year reign?

Well you have to look as far back as Peter Stringfellow's city-based King Mojo Club and Terry Thornton's Esquire (in the building now occupied by the The Leadmill) to trace the beginnings: both were frequented by future Limit-owners George Webster and Kevan Johnson. Years later they were to take the very best of both venues and, to coin a phrase they nicked from The Eagles, took things 'to the limit'. DJ George Webster and ex-policeman Kevan Johnson didn't, on the face of it, make for the likeliest rock'n'roll partnership but, as it turns out, theirs was an absolutely essential one to get the new venue up and running.

New nightclub licences were an absolute nightmare to secure in Sheffield in the seventies (a situation which became synonymous with Steel City for decades). Following the approval of the one for The Limit, there wasn't much else granted until The Republic secured its licence in the mid-1990s, the club which eventually evolved into international hit Gatecrasher.

Obviously having friends in the force wouldn't have hampered the new partners' bid for a licence from the relevant authorities: Johnson was an ex-cop himself.

George Webster, on the other hand, more than ticked the rock'n'roll boxes - he was already a veritable veteran of the city's music scene and had already built a strong following via long-standing DJ stints at legendary city-centre rock bars The Buccaneer and The Wapentake, the latter better known now as The Casbah.

He'd also proved his worth at picking a winner: years earlier George had started promoting bands at the age of 14 and he booked Joe Cocker (then a fledgling Vance Arnold fronting his Avengers) at Sheffield's Meersbrook Vestry Hall in 1963.

"It was Sheffield's equivalent of CBGB – it was the place where things happened." In fact if The Limit had opened two years earlier, on the cusp of the first wave of punk, there might not have been a CBGB at all...

The partners' had to find a site for The Limit which could fill the well-publicised gap in the market for a live-music venue to cater for acts too small for Sheffield City Hall but too big for your average pub. Their choice was genius.

It was dark, dank and had subterranean rebellion written all over it.

The Limit occupied 72-82 West Street and sat in the basement of a shopping precinct.

If New York's CBGB – heralded as the birth place of much of the punk rock movement - had fancied relocating to Sheffield, it would have killed for the place.

Mark Albrow of Sheffield band Hula agrees.

"It was Sheffield's equivalent of CBGB – it was the place where things happened." In fact if The Limit had opened two years earlier, on the cusp of the first wave of punk, there might not have been a CBGB at all...

Photo: Bailey Brothers

CHAPTER ONE

Setting the scene

THE CLASH AND PACKING PEAS AT BACHELORS

Sheffield's count on the punk rock band success front might have been less than zero in the anarchic explosion that ricocheted across the county in 1976 but it did have one claim to fame – it was home to the first ever live performance of The Clash.

Joe Strummer's fledgling outfit supported the Sex Pistols at Snig Hill's Black Swan on July 4, 1976.

He wasn't, by all accounts, looking his best that night.

Clive Porter, former schoolfriend of Human League front man Phil Oakey and a man who was soon to be working alongside future ABC front man Martin Fry on the line at Bachelors Peas in Hillsborough to boost his university grant income, said: "We were always on the lookout for new music and something to happen and I'd already previously caught the 101ers [Strummer's last band] in Sheffield. That night this scruffy bloke shuffled in our direction and I expected him to start begging as he looked homeless. It was actually Joe Strummer wandering around telling people they were about to play."

Though there weren't as many people at the gig as later claimed to be there - a million-or-so also sought early punk kudos in claiming to have been at the Sex Pistols' gig at the Free Trade Hall in Manchester - the Black Swan appearance still merits a pretty impressive place in Sheffield's music heritage.

Joe Strummer, recounting the Snig Hill gig years later to Mojo, said: "It was great. At least I think it was good. I'm not sure... We made a few screw-ups. It was the first time Paul Simonon was on stage and so forth. We actually managed to play the

"Clash were just a cacophonous barrage of noise... It's enough to turn you on to Demis Roussos."

tunes. It was highly entertaining. There were punks even in Sheffield at that moment. It was a Sunday and 200 people turned up. They were very receptive."

That certainly wasn't the view of everyone that night.

The verdict of one "anonymous music lover, Sheffield" on the NME letters page a few days later said: "Clash were just a cacophonous barrage of noise...

"It's enough to turn you on to Demis Roussos".

Photo: David Richardson collection

The Black Swan in the late 1960s

Whether that was penned by a member of The Damned, who were in a race to release 'the' first punk single, we'll probably never know. They won anyway: New Rose was released on October 22, 1976, with Anarchy In the UK by the Sex Pistols following up on November 26, 1976.

"I only recognised a few locals in the place. The majority of people were from London and they were sitting in the middle of the floor."

Clive Porter argued that the actual Sheffield contingent would have been lucky to get into double figures in Steel City that night of July 4.

He said: "I only recognised a few locals in the place. The majority of people were from London and they were sitting on chairs in the middle of the floor."

Two people who definitely weren't there that night were future Limit club operators George Webster and Kevan Johnson.

Johnson would probably have been welcomed with a hail of vomit – he was still a copper at this point - while George Webster had already written off the live music scene in the city. Webster said at the time: "When the Mojo and Esquire Club shut in the sixties, that was the end of Sheffield as far as any kind of live scene was concerned."

He doesn't mention the regular gigs put on by both Sheffield University and Sheffield Polytechnic, both of which staged performances by most of the punk/new wave bands that blitzed the charts from late '76 onwards, but these never had an open-door policy as far as non-students were concerned.

Unfortunately, even hosting a seminal gig by The Clash doesn't secure a venue's future.

The Black Swan was shut within weeks and a gaping hole was left in Sheffield's live music scene...

Mojo owner Peter Stringfellow at the Mojo Christmas party 1984

Photo Sheffield Newspapers

Poster for the Mojo

BEAUTIFUL
MOJO CLUB
SHEFFIELD
SUN. 17th SEPT.
ALL DAY RAVE!
THE
ONLY 10/-
AMEN CORNER
CHART TOPPERS
DISC: 'GIN HOUSE'
Coming! U.S.As. Little
STEVIE WONDER!

Keeping the riff raff in

The UK's after-dark scene was still acclimatising to the shock of punk rock and its more toned down new wave counterpart when George Webster and Kevan Johnson first started plotting The Limit in the dawn of 1977.

Antiquated collar-and-tie dress codes (a dictum which was later turned on its head at The Limit) were very much in vogue at established nightclubs and did a sterling job of keeping the riff raff out of the way of the new alternative types.

But it did little for the new breed of punk rockers and art-school fashionistas eager to show their mettle.

The tabloids were doing an admirable job of fanning the flames on the back of Bill Grundy's goading of the Sex Pistols on their infamous appearance on Thames TV's early evening news programme Today a couple of years earlier (it was aired on December 1, 1976), and 'shock horror punk rocker ate my hamster' stories still boosted newspaper sales nicely

The blame for all this so-called civil unrest could hardly be laid firmly at the door of youth culture gone bananas.

The Yorkshire Ripper was busy wasting the region's prostitute community – a situation that would soon have women of all professions too scared witless to go out on their own after dark.

Jim Callahan's Government was in turmoil as strikes kicked off right, left and centre with the country nicely counting down to the Winter of Discontent.

In fact, only one man seemed to keep the UK from mass genocide in early 1978, one John Travolta.

Mindless escapism was in full swing thanks to his Saturday Night Fever hit released in the States in December 1977 but nothing – not even Jaws II which was also set to do the rounds - could prepare the nation for the hysteria which would surround Grease.

Travolta, together with the Grease look, the dances, the finger-pointing and fashions spanning everything from white suits to fifties' quiffs, wiped the floor with everything and everybody that year (except one-time Limit-goer Bob Geldof, who knocked John Travolta and Olivia Newton John off the top spot with Rat Trap when fronting the Boomtown Rats).

Nowhere was the Travolta influence felt more acutely than in Sheffield's Josephines nightclub in Barkers Pool which had been opened in 1976 by self-made multi-millionaire local boy Dave Allen, a former big-band leader who was already running the money-spinning Napoleons Casino a couple of miles out of the city centre on Ecclesall Road.

Photo: Sheffield Newspapers

The Sex Pistols at Radio Hallam in January 1976

Josephines Birthday Party (left to right), Maggie Hardwick, Dave Allen and son Mark who ran the club

Photo: Sheffield Newspapers

Allen stuck two fingers up at the nascent punk rockers when Josephines opened with champagne glitz, wine bar and baby grand piano and he carried on with the clean-image door policy: the club was a massive hit from day one but punk rockers weren't allowed within spitting-distance of the door. Josephines did a roaring trade for quarter of a century.

But the scene certainly wasn't all doom and gloom if you were slightly alternative in your outlook in Sheffield in 1978. The Top Rank and Sheffield City Hall provided room-a-plenty for bigger gigs with both Sheffield University and Sheffield Polytechnic bringing up the rear.

The Limit management too went on to promote big, money-spinning gigs at The Top Rank and probably went a long way to persuading Kevan Johnson and George Webster to purchase the Lyceum building, which many say was the beginning of their downfall.

Allen stuck two fingers up to the nascent punk rockers when Josephines opened with champagne glitz.

It certainly wasn't all doom and gloom if you were slightly alternative in your outlook

Staff and customers from the North of England's first punk rock fashion shop which opened on Sheffield's Ecclesall Road in 1977

Photo: Sheffield Newspapers

The Mojo Club being demolished
Photo: Sheffield Newspapers

CHAPTER TWO

The Buccaneer, the Wapentake Bar...

AND THE FUTURE PATRON SAINT OF **HEAVY METAL**

Olga Marshall, the resplendent and formidable manager of two of the city's most legendary rock and alternative bars, played her own pivotal role in the early days of The Limit.

Her employment of George Webster as a DJ at Leopold Street's long-gone Buccaneer Bar (which ran from 1968 to 1973 under the long-gone Grand Hotel as a collection of themed bars) and then Wapentake Bar (still rocking today as The Casbah on Wellington Street) helped him to secure an ardent following of future Limit-goers years later and to build the confidence and contacts to open his own venue.

Olga Marshall in her Buccaneer Bar early days

Photo: Sheffield Newspapers

Running Sheffield's foremost rock/alternative bars was probably never part of the grand master plan of hotel-owners Trust House Forte but they probably didn't realise what a formidable force they'd set on downstairs when Olga Marshall first arrived as a lowly barmaid in 1964, a woman who was to become as near as the city would ever get to a patron saint of heavy metal.

Sheffield-born Olga, now 82 and still unsure why her parents gave her a Russian first name, was never happy with the way things were going at The Buccaneer in the early days.

She said: "We'd only got a jukebox so I spoke to the management company about getting a DJ in. They brought in a company called DRM, I think, who came along with flashing lights and the full set-up but they just weren't what we wanted at all.

"I asked if I could sort something out myself and I found George Webster, who was playing at Cannon Hall social club at Page Hall [Sheffield] at the time, and he started playing the kind of music that my customers liked.

"We took more on our first night with George than The Buccaneer took on its average weekend."

It's fair to say that Olga started to get her own way after that and she also began to build a strong bond with George Webster.

Trust House Forte presented Olga with a bunch of flowers after George's first night on the turntables but the management never really quite understood the rock/alternative crowd (except via their wallets of course).

The Buccaneer became one of the city's busiest venues with Olga at the helm, a woman who was already a mother of four in 1972 and who didn't smoke and rarely drank. It was a massive concern with around 60 staff.

George Webster was soon doing far more than just DJing and, alongside Olga, started becoming a regular fixture in the local press.

He was happy to pose as Long John Silver and even helped organise a much-publicised charity drive, alongside his fellow DJs, to collect food for senior citizens at Christmas.

"We decided we would try and show that young people do care about the old folk. We went round collecting and nobody refused to give," he said at the time.

It was George's idea together with fellow DJ Ian Roberts, who also worked under the moniker 'Cisco Sounds'.

Buccaneer Bar regular Peter Eales said: "There was nowhere else playing music like it in Sheffield. You went to The Buccaneer if you wanted to hear stuff that was different,

Photo: Sheffield Newspapers

Buccaneer assistant manager Norman Coldwell (left), DJs Ian Roberts (right) and George Webster (middle)

Captain's Cabin Bar re-launch ceremony

Photo: Sheffield Newspapers

that wasn't mainstream. It had a real buzz about it. There were lots of different rooms but it was that dark you could never tell where you were anyway."

The buzz didn't last.

Trust House Forte sold the site for redevelopment and, despite outlasting the Grand Hotel upstairs which was bulldozed and replaced by an office block a few weeks earlier, The Buccaneer shut its doors for the last time in 1973 after 1,979 days of custom.

Aware of the widespread dismay at the thought of closure among the hardcore following, the management made the decision to close the bars without warning in a bid to stop souvenir hunters.

"But despite this the police are still looking for four missing tables," it was reported in the Sheffield Star.

One of those tables still sits in the corner of Olga Marshall's garage along with The Buccaneer sign: where the other three are we'll probably never know.

George Webster poses as Long John Silver

"There were lots of different rooms but it was that dark you could never tell where you were anyway."

Scenes at the Buccaneer Bar

Olga Marshall (foreground) and Buccaneer Bar staff

Photo: Olga Marshall collection

Enter Wapentake Bar

Thankfully the rockers weren't left to drown their sorrows in bottles of Newcastle Brown on the barren streets of Sheffield for long: help was at hand in the shape of another bar that was punching well below its weight for Trust House Forte in the city.

They called on the only person capable of rescuing the situation at the Wapentake Bar underneath their Grosvenor House Hotel in 1973 – Olga Marshall.

She toed the company line for the first few months with less of a rock outlook and most of The Buccaneer regulars decamped to Crazy Daisy on High Street, the venue made famous as the club in which Human League front man Phil Oakey first clapped eyes on Joanne Catherall and Susan Sulley, who went on to complete his new-look band and go on to global domination.

After a few months, Trust House Forte management relented and George "Buccaneer" Webster – as he was billed at the time - and his music became the new Wapentake Bar residents.

Management at the Grosvenor House Hotel were actually eager to do their bit to help welcome their new rock crowd.

"The hotel manager, Mr Tallis, suggested we ought to have a party for the rockers and he offered to lay on some jelly," said Olga.

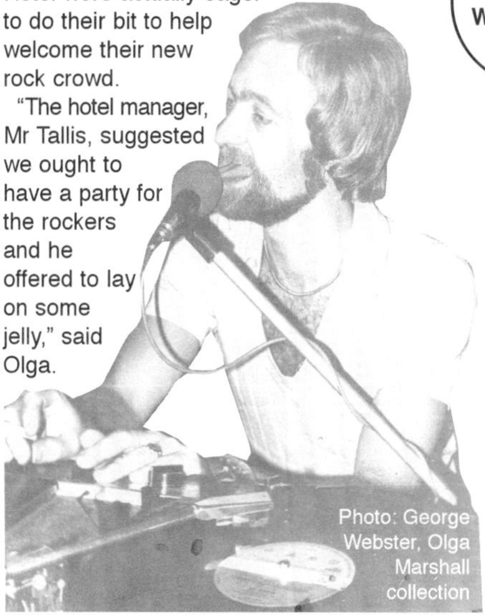

Photo: George Webster, Olga Marshall collection

"I told him not to be so stupid. He did take his suit off one night, came down in a T-shirt and told me: 'Your crowd are actually alright to talk to.' I'm not quite sure what he expected!"

As with The Buccaneer, as the takings increased, interference from the hotel upstairs decreased.

Entrance to the Wapentake Bar

Few people would ever associate the then swish Grosvenor House Hotel (the place still survives but is ear-marked for demolition to make way for a heavily delayed shopping precinct) on Charter Square roundabout in the city centre as the landlord of the Wapentake. It probably worked better that way: only the management and a few others knew the two were inherently linked; it would have done little for the street cred of either operation had the situation been otherwise.

But the place did have a true "Jekyll and Hyde" persona in its early days according to former manager Steve Bolderson who went on to become a manager at The Limit.

Photo: Sheffield Newspapers

Olga Marshall (left), one-time Limit manager Paul Farrett (bow tie) and George Webster (right) at Wapentake Bar

"It was a rock bar by night and a restaurant by day. We'd take the curtains down and move the tables out for 6.30pm every night for the rockers," he laughed.

Wapentake Bar had its own entrance, out of view of the hotel and you had to descend a flight of stairs before you got so much as a sniff of the action. (Things weren't that dissimilar to The Limit, all told, and George Webster probably drew plenty of inspiration from the venue.) Décor was – at best – basic; it had a very low ceiling and the place was sweaty and dark.

The punters couldn't have been happier and the place was soon running seven nights a week and was also promoting regular gigs - Def Leppard played one of their first ever outings down there. The bar soon became legendary on the UK rock scene.

It was also the training ground for future Limit DJ Paul Unwin, who started working for George Webster at the Wapentake.

Ladies Clubs and Committees . . .

Have a pleasant day at the Wapentake— including guided tour of the Grosvenor House Hotel followed by Lunch at The Wapentake Bar and a choice of 3 films at the Cineplex.

Phone MRS. MARSHALL on 20041.

Morning Coffee available from 10.30 a.m. daily in

THE WAPENTAKE BAR

Hot and cold Lunches 11.30 a.m.-2.30 p.m.

Wapentake Bar's daylight hours alter-ego

"It was a rock bar by night and a restaurant by day. We'd take the curtains down and move the tables out for 6.30pm every night for the rockers."

Future Limit DJ Paul Unwin spins the discs at Wapentake Bar

There was rarely trouble, despite the venue's appeal to biker gangs whom the firm hand of Olga Marshall always managed to control – and it was always renowned for its almost 'family atmosphere.'

But Wapentake Bar was always firmly rock and, though they used to frequent the place, it never had the same resonance for the punks and new wave fraternity which was appearing from 1976.

Paul Unwin said: "In the mid seventies we did begin to move away from rock with the advent of punk. I can remember the landlady Olga Marshall taking exception to the fact that people were turning up dressed in bin bags with little bum flaps.

"But for me it was the way forward. I was only 21 but the music scene was really beginning to excite me again.

"It had been in a bit of a trough after 1972 because it went into the glam stages of Bolan and Sweet while hard rock acts like Deep Purple and Led Zeppelin played music of the same quality as they'd done previously."

Wapentake Bar became a way of life for many people. It definitely changed the life of Northern General Hospital worker Vernon Price.

"I don't know if you could call 6/7 nights a week being a regular – I guess he was!" said Paul Unwin.

Music-mad Vernon spent his time requesting tracks from Paul Unwin and later did the odd DJ stint at The Limit as well as gaining the nickname 'Tommy The Tiler' as he also tiled the venue.

"Vernon was a customer with a very acute taste in music," says Paul.

Nobody could fail to miss the amount of money the Wapentake Bar was turning over – it was, like The Buccaneer – a formidable operation on the Sheffield bar scene.

With the punk market going begging and Kevan Johnson already having a strong friendship with George Webster at the Wapentake, plans for a new venue started moving at a rapid pace.

"Nobody could believe it was run by this smartly dressed mother of four who took no nonsense from anyone."

Olga Marshall in Wapentake Bar early days

Photo: Sheffield Newspapers

Olga Marshall was asked if she fancied jumping ship and running the new operation being planned.

"I didn't know anything about it until George Webster asked to see me one night and asked if I wanted to come and work for him," said Olga. "I said no – the hours were too late. I liked pub hours rather than the 2am of nightclubs and said I wanted to stay at Wapentake Bar."

Thousands upon thousands of rockers over the next two decades were thankful she stayed.

Regular Ian Cheetham said:

"Wapentake Bar became an absolute magnet for rockers – if you were in Sheffield you had to go to The Wap.

"I was a punter there for nearly two decades and nobody could believe it was run by this smartly dressed mother of four who took no nonsense from anyone – Hells Angels or anyone."

Future Limit DJ Paul Unwin looking very un-punk rock at Wapentake Bar in 1975 Paul Unwin collection

Olga Marshall's proudest moment was probably a return visit by Def Leppard, who performed for her one more time at Wapentake Bar on October 5, 1995, in front of most of the world's music press

Photos: Sheffield Newspapers/ Olga Marshall collection

CHAPTER THREE

Siouxsie Sioux

and BITTER SUITE unveil The LIMIT

Although The Limit didn't actually open until punk was well into its second year, the initial idea had probably been buzzing around in George Webster's head for years.

He was in a better position than most to make a success of things. Webster already had the following from The Buccaneer and Wapentake Bar but punk rock wasn't being catered for at The Wap and there was also that gap in the market for a venue catering for smaller bands following the closure of the Black Swan.

But it takes a lot more than spinning a few discs to open, run and manage a successful venue and that's where Kevan Johnson came in.

As well as being an ex-policeman, Johnson also knew the licensing trade because his dad had run pubs in Heeley and Woodseats for years.

Photo: Sheffield Newspapers

Limit entrance in the early days

"We had a meeting and decided to look at some premises and luckily enough we found some straight away on West Street."

Kevan said: "One night in early 1977, I went into Wapentake Bar and bumped into George Webster who was DJing. I noticed how many people were outside queuing to get inside and listen to the music he was playing because there were no venues around then playing that type of music. I just casually mentioned that, despite all this demand, there wasn't another venue kids could go dressed in jeans and a T-shirt, like you could at the old Mojo club where we all used to go.

"We had a meeting and decided to look at some premises and luckily enough we found some straight away on West Street."

George Webster said there was only one other place in the running – the old Abbeydale Picture House on Abbeydale Road.

Kevan Johnson said that, for all his background knowledge, obtaining a licence for their idea was a nightmare. "Things were very difficult getting the licence – we had to fight tooth and nail. We had to play on the fact we were a different concept."

Wapentake Bar manager Steve Bolderson said that Kevan Johnson was in a better position than most to land one, which wasn't surprising given his background.

He said: "I think Kevan's father had some influence in the licensing trade."

Kevan Johnson and George Webster got planning permission for The Limit in April 1977.

The venue, a 5,000 square feet area in the basement of a West Street shopping precinct, was going to cost £30,000 and boast disco, restaurant, wine bar, bars, mobile stage and a capacity for around 350.

But the licence had a strict condition attached to it, according to George Webster. The aftermath of the infamous Bill Grundy interview and the furore surrounding the Sex Pistols was very evident at the hearing.

"When I went to the licensing court the chairman thanked me for a fantastic presentation and said 'I've now got a new outlook on what modern music is all about and I'm really enlightened but I'd just like to say we grant it on the understanding that you will never, ever book the Sex Pistols.'"

New city night club ready to open tonight

SHEFFIELD licensing justices have given the go-ahead for a new nightclub in the town.

The club, The Limit, is in the basement of the old West End shopping precinct, in West Street, and will open tonight, provided the premises pass an inspection by the fire brigade this afternoon.

The justices granted a music, singing and dancing licence with supper and special hours certificates.

Mr. Kevan Johnson, aged 29, will be running the club with his partner, rock DJ George Webster.

Mr. Johnson told The Star: "We will be playing rock music records by bands that never release a single, but sell millions of LPs like Led Zeppelin, Pink Floyd and so on." He added that people wearing jeans will be allowed in.

There will be a restaurant with room for 100. The club is due to open tonight with a live group, Bitter Sweet.

Webster and Johnson – both 28 years old at the time – were initially aiming for September 1977 to be open for business, a date that turned out to be rather optimistic.

One of their main arguments in proving a need for The Limit and landing the necessary licences was the demand for live acts which were too small to fill the nearby Sheffield City Hall, whose Oval Hall boasted a capacity of over 2,000 but which would cater for 1,000 and still look busy if you shut the two-tier balcony.

Webster was also scathing of the dress-codes demanded by the city's mainstream venues and the need to offer an alternative. He said: "All the clubs are stereotyped. You have got to look as though you are going to a wedding to get in. Kids don't like that, they like to dress according to the trend."

Once they realised they were never going to be ready for September 1977 they lined up January 17, 1978, as the new date for opening.

As is regularly the case where nightlife venues are concerned when there are the stringent rules of everyone from planning to the fire authority to meet, The Limit failed to meet that target opening date as well.

It didn't seem to cause too much of an issue as neither dates were widely publicised. There were certainly no complaints when the club did finally open: the two partners' concept was delivered, virtually to the letter, and was the complete antithesis of everything else that was going on in town.

Luxury décor didn't figure, dress-code was set to be non-existent (unless you turned up in a suit and you'd perhaps be turned away) and it was all about the music doing the talking and cementing the image.

Kevan Johnson said at the time: "We're after a club which can generate some kind of excitement through music.

"We want people to come down and get a kick out of it. We're not aiming for anything luxurious – just a place to play the best music."

But there was also a note of caution from George Webster, who realised they needed to keep their options open in case things didn't go entirely to plan and they had to diversify to keep afloat.

He said: "It's going to be a rock club. That covers a multitude but it probably means we'll be playing soul music only at lunchtimes."

The Limit passed its afternoon inspection by the fire service with flying colours on March 22, 1978, and prepared to open that night.

Nerves must have been at breaking point before the doors opened. They might have got one of the best positions in the city centre for capturing passing-trade, being in a key part of the popular 'West Street run', but anyone who has ever run a nightclub knows there are no dead-certs with the after-dark industry.

But any air of trepidation for DJ Paul Unwin – who was leaving relatively secure employment at

Wapentake Bar to provide the sounds at the new Limit venue but actually ended up running himself ragged working both venues for the first few weeks of The Limit's life – would soon be replaced by the adrenalin rush of first-night nerves as the minutes counted down to opening.

Bitter Suite – popular club band that were the stars of opening night.

Many people think Siouxsie and the Banshees played the opening night at The Limit but they couldn't be further from the truth: the venue played things rather safer and decided against the chance of the punks tearing their nice new club apart on day one.

It was actually local club-act Bitter Suite who packed the place.

TONIGHT!!
"BITTER SUITE"
(on stage at 9.30)
THE FIRST BAND TO APPEAR AT SHEFFIELD'S NEWEST NIGHT LIFE
THE LIMIT
WEST STREET
THEN ON THURSDAY
"WE'RE GONNA GIVE YA
THE PUSH"
(on stage at 9.30)
THE BEST DISCO MUSIC YOU'VE EVER HEARD – FROM THE OLD BUCCANEER HIMSELF
GEORGE WEBSTER
+
SATURDAY LUNCH & NIGHT
"WYRE"
(DENIMS OKAY)

Paul Unwin, who was The Limit manager as well as its main DJ, said: "Opening night was a total disaster but the customers wouldn't have known that. We'd come as DJs but we were now asked to be night-club managers.

"We were trying to get the beer to switch on and the lights to switch off."

Paul Neilson, a Sheffield University student at the time, said: "I remember going down on opening night and there was a true excitement about the place. I wasn't a Bitter Suite fan but the place was absolutely rammed at the opening and I had to say they put on a good show.

"The place had a real feel of rebellion and somewhere that was set to offer a home for people who didn't want to go to Josephines or the more trendy places."

Gerry Scanlan, bass player for Bitter Suite, said they ended up with an unexpected audience of tradesmen for their soundcheck.

"I can remember arriving at the gig for the sound-check in the afternoon to find joiners and electricians etc still working and the place was opening in a few hours !!!

"When we came back in the evening they were putting the finishing touches to the place just before people came in. The queue outside was enormous....... when we went out on to the stage all you could see was a sea of faces stretching the length and width of the club and right up to the front of the stage."

Paul Unwin confirms that Siouxsie appeared soon after along with other bands about to break into the big-time.

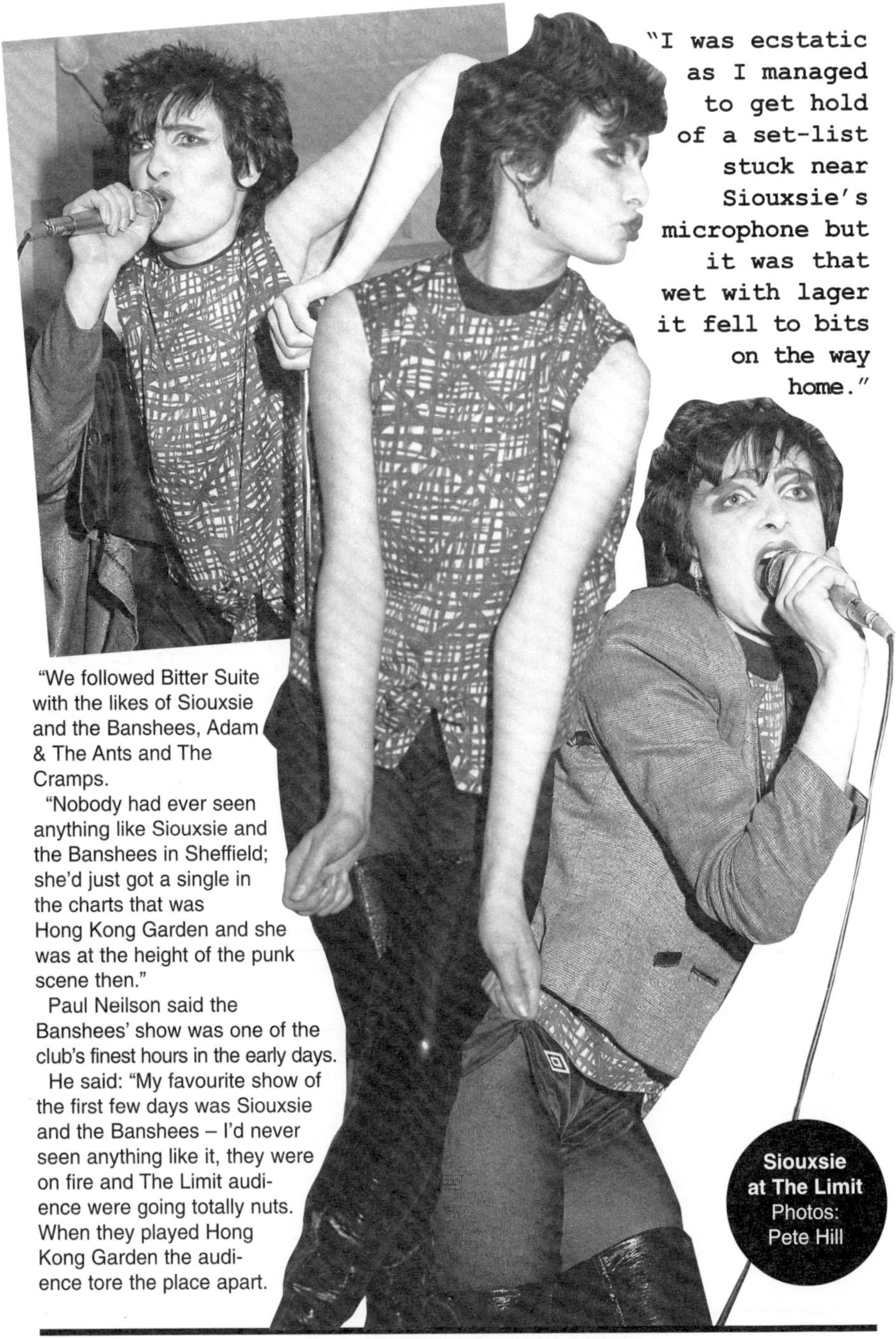

"I was ecstatic as I managed to get hold of a set-list stuck near Siouxsie's microphone but it was that wet with lager it fell to bits on the way home."

"We followed Bitter Suite with the likes of Siouxsie and the Banshees, Adam & The Ants and The Cramps.

"Nobody had ever seen anything like Siouxsie and the Banshees in Sheffield; she'd just got a single in the charts that was Hong Kong Garden and she was at the height of the punk scene then."

Paul Neilson said the Banshees' show was one of the club's finest hours in the early days.

He said: "My favourite show of the first few days was Siouxsie and the Banshees – I'd never seen anything like it, they were on fire and The Limit audience were going totally nuts. When they played Hong Kong Garden the audience tore the place apart.

Siouxsie at The Limit
Photos: Pete Hill

Photo: Pete Hill

The Push (with future soap star Ray Ashcroft far right) who were lined up to perform on the second night

" I was near the front and I remember being totally drenched in sweat. I was ecstatic as I managed to get hold of a set-list stuck near Siouxsie's microphone but it was that wet with lager it fell to bits on the way home. I nearly cried!"

Andy Smith, Def Leppard's first roadie, said: "My favourite Limit night wasn't the Lepps funnily enough (too busy working - a roadie's life never stops). No, that'd be Siouxsie and the Banshees. The gang had been to see Thin Lizzy at the City Hall on their 'Thunder and Lightning' tour. Came out and wandered to the 51 stop - only to see a queue outside the Limit. Pleased to learn that Siouxsie was on so we saw that too. And I got up for work next day. And I wasn't late.

"And I had change from a tenner. Eee lad, them were t' days...."

Sheffield's own band The Push – fronted by Ray Ashcroft, who was to become far better known as an actor starring in The Bill and Emmerdale – were actually the first punk act to perform at The Limit.

They lined up to play the second night (March 23, 1978).

Occasional Limit DJ Vernon Price said some of the initial shows were absolutely amazing and a true first for Sheffield: "Bands like The Cramps and B-52s were playing awesome music and totally different to anything anyone had ever seen. I'd be with the bands from when they were loading in and I was very impressed with the way they went about their business.

"They'd just take their coats off and get on with it. They'd do their sound-check, have a bite to eat, have a couple of drinks at the bar and then go on and blow the place apart."

The Limit was into its stride within days and was soon building an enviable reputation for booking bands about to break into the big-time.

Paul Unwin said: "When Adam & The Ants appeared they'd done the Jubilee concert in 1977 but Adam wasn't famous then.

"We went into a bit of a lull after the first few days because we didn't know which direction to go. But then the city's student population took us on board and we started with an agency in London booking the bands."

"He'd had a single out, Deutscher Girls, but it had never been picked up by the radio stations. BBC Radio One didn't know what to do with punk – they didn't know whether to accept it or wash their hands of it and look for something else.

"If you'd have seen Adam & The Ants then, you'd have realised they were going to be a very, very big band. His stage presence was exceptional and although the band didn't sound that musical they were very talented in what they were doing."

Paul Neilson remembers Adam & The Ants well. "I don't think I missed a gig in the first few weeks and this one clearly stands out. My mum paid for my ticket as it landed just before my birthday in late April: I was 19.

"There was already a huge buzz starting to build about the band and I was one of the first through the door that night; I remember because the floor was spotless and I remember it being covered in glasses as I left - I was one of the last ones to go as I was trying to get a T-shirt."

Because The Limit didn't have a strict dress-code it had far more freedom to try out new kinds of nights in the city centre catering for different crowds. Everything from a folk night to regular reggae slots became part of the early roster.

Kevan Johnson admits they were soon a quandary as to what direction to take the club in.

"We went into a bit of a lull after the first few days because we didn't know which direction to go. But then the city's student population took us on board and we started with an agency in London booking the bands."

George Webster said Bitter Suite was more a VIP night for friends and associates with, as far as he was concerned, Siouxsie and the Banshees as the official 'public' opening.

Limit folk

SHEFFIELD'S new Limit rock club is going folksy.

From next month folk nights are to be staged on Mondays at the West Street venue with three artists a week.

Bizarre jug band Cocky, last year's Melody Maker Folk/Rock Contest winners Six Hands in Tempo and compere John Leonard will get the new feature under way on June 19.

Richard Digance, Hedgeho Pie, the John Renbour Band and the Bothy Ban are future attraction

THE LIMIT
WEST STREET
PHONE 730940
TONIGHT
LOCAL BAND
THE HUMAN LEAGUE
Admission 20p
Tuesday night
DAYS OF GRACE
Admission 60p
Wednesday night
STARS OF THE ALBUM JUBILEE!!!!
ADAM AND THE ANTS
(Be early)
Admission 60p

CHAPTER FOUR

A launch pad

FOR SHEFFIELD'S **ELECTRO-DOMINANCE** OF THE EIGHTIES

There's no doubt that The Limit played a key part in developing and helping break some of Sheffield's most important bands of the late 1970s and 1980s.

It opened in the throes of one of the most creative periods in Steel City's music history and helped drive the burgeoning electronic scene.

When it wasn't staging the gigs, its DJs were regularly the first to be playing the records fresh from the pressing plants.

Human League and Def Leppard

Paul Unwin said: "I remember Martyn Ware bringing Empire State Human into the club – it must have been the first time it had been played.

"I never even bothered listening to it beforehand. I just stuck it on the turntable and played it. The whole club danced.The whole club went out and bought it and were right behind The Human League."

The Limit offered numerous free-entry showcase gigs in its early days to get the punters in and help develop local talent. George Webster confirmed that The Limit management often considered going further in terms of their involvement with key acts – management of Def Leppard was once muted.

September 11, 1978 was one of the more bizarre line-ups in Sheffield's musical history. It was the one and only time future multi-million album-selling rock monsters Def Leppard supported rising electro-stars Human League in day one of a two-day free local music festival.

The Human League

Photo: Glenn Gregory

Graph, Ton Trick and/or Monitors (nobody seems quite sure which of these two actually played) were sandwiched between the two acts that went on to global domination. (Day two of the soiree didn't produce any more Sheffield music legends unfortunately.)

Gary Wilson: "George Webster, in his infinite wisdom, booked Def Leppard on the same bill as Human League. The League turned up with all these synthesisers or whatever and then produced all these Perspex screens which they then put round the synths. I asked what they were for and they said they were expecting trouble that night. Sure enough, because it was a rock audience, the glasses starting flying at them."

Human League were already used to a hostile reaction in some quarters: they'd even considered crash helmets at one point.

A previous gig supporting punk act The Rezillos (which included future Human League member Jo Callis in the line-up) in London had prompted band member Ian Marsh to put together a greenhouse-resembling bunch of Perspex screens to protect his synthesizer from flying missiles for the first time.The Limit show was only Def Leppard's third proper gig. Martyn Ware of Human League (and later Heaven 17) wasn't particularly complimentary of the performances of either act that night. "Def Leppard were abysmal but probably so were we. The main thing I remember about them, apart from the music being so completely derivative and rubbish, was that the lead singer was not very good.

"He came on stage, stripped to the waist, with skin tight loon pants and the biggest wooden black cross I've ever seen in my life hanging round his neck. Monty Python couldn't have done it better."

Phil Oakey saw more hope for the fledgling Leppard.

"Def Leppard were pretty obviously serious from the start. Of all the bands around I think they were the ones that knew exactly what they were doing. I was never dismissive of them."

Limit owners George Webster and Kevan Johnson were quite happy with Def Leppard because they already had a strong following, which meant plenty of cash over the bar.

Def Leppard bassist Rick Savage remembers the outing well. The whole band ended up becoming regulars at the club.

"The Limit more or less coincided with our band starting out. I was seventeen and I was just about old enough to go and drink in bars.

Def Leppard

Photo: Sheffied Newspapers

"My first experience of going in there was when there was a free concert for all local bands that George Webster and Kevan Johnson had put on – there were around ten bands on.

"We were the only heavy metal band on the bill – it wasn't the time for hard rock as it was right at the top of the punk era or it was more art-schooly. People would laugh if you were starting a hard rock band.

"I remember thinking 'how can they [Human League] be any good, they've not even got a drummer'. Little did we know that years later we'd go down the same route with sequencing and bringing that into the hard rock genre.

"I thought The Limit was absolutely brilliant. You have to remember that at that time there were night-clubs in the typical sense of the word, like the old Genevieve or Josephines, clubs you couldn't get into with jeans on; then The Limit came along and broke a lot of rules. It was so refreshing as a place. It wasn't a disco: it was a bar where bands played.

"It was grubby but there was a certain vibe about it and, to my knowledge, it was one of the first of its kind.

"We went down a storm because most of the audience were our friends and it was an open house [free to get in]. We kind of stole the show for that reason and Kevan and George immediately said 'we'll book you'. We came back and headlined.

"The week before we headlined Kevan barred Steve Clarke, our guitarist, and another of us. There was an altercation in the club, everyone had had too much to drink, and Steve – god love him – stood out and he got thrown up the stairs.

"He shouted: 'You can't bar me I'm playing here next week.' So they let him back in!

"Once you'd played there and you got to know George and Kevan it became a nice place to go and we genuinely liked it. It was cheap beer and after hours and there were the old arcade games, like Pac Man, there. We'd go every Friday night regularly.

"It was hard rock and punk and everything in between. It was a really cool place to hang out.

"I think there were a few question marks around the first time we played down there. We ended up with about 800 people in there and walked out with £50! And we thought, 'hang on a minute – something's not right here'. "The dressing room was more like an overgrown wardrobe but that was part of the vibe of the place. It was crap but it was all part of the charm.

"When you look back you've got to be thankful for a place like The Limit. We didn't want to go down the route of playing Working Men's Clubs.

"It gave bands like us a chance and punters a chance to see new bands. There was just something special about The Limit."

"When you look back you've got to be thankful for a place like The Limit. We didn't want to go down the route of playing Working Men's Clubs. It gave bands like us a chance and punters a chance to see new bands. There was just something special about The Limit."

Cabaret Voltaire

An early Cabaret Voltaire gig at The Limit was marked by a gang of skinheads threatening to give them a good hiding.

The attitude of Limit owners George Webster and Kevan Johnson didn't help, according to the band.

Chris Watson said: "We had agreed a payment but they said they weren't going to pay us that. They said we'd get a share of the bar takings instead. So we just set up this loop of white noise or whatever and went to the bar."

Photo: Rod Siddall

Cabaret Voltaire at the Russell club in Hulme

In fairness it seemed to work in their favour. Audience member that night Mark Albrow said: "I first saw the Cabs at The Limit. I was struck by the fact that they weren't insisting they were the centre of attention.

"They weren't even on the stage. It was mesmerising"

Chris Peach: "I remember going to see Cabaret Voltaire and Mal announcing the next song as 'No Escape'. Phil Oakey shouted 'This is when they lock the doors'."

Clock DVA

Clock DVA actually made their live debut at The Limit on July 25 1978, supporting Human League.

The line-up consisted of Adi Newton on vocals and treatments, Jud on bass, guitar and vocals, and Joseph Hurst on synth, with percussion and noise on reel-to-reel.

They certainly made an impression with a haphazard set with a bit of violence and

Clock DVA

Photo: Pete Hill

destruction thrown in for good measure. The Limit banned them.

Mirror Crack'D member Phil Staniland said Clock DVA became very aloof the minute they set foot in The Limit.

"They seemed to adopt this strange code where they'd only talk to women. They practised in a room next to us and we always chatted to them in the sandwich shop but they totally blanked us when they were in The Limit."

Comsat Angels

One of the city's most enduring bands played The Limit on various occasions.

Comsat Angels first played the venue in an earlier guise as Skylids and Radio Earth.

They were already quite accomplished musicians with roots that can be traced right back to two Rotherham bands – Mrs Tibbets and Spider – that first started playing around 1971.

In 1978 Radio Earth were spotted by Radar Records, then home to Elvis Costello.

Their first major gig that followed was supporting Pere Ubu in Newcastle.

Steve Fellows said: "It was an absolute disaster. We were abysmal and the agent and Frank [their London-based manager] said 'you're shit and we're going'."

They were soon back with a new name, The Comsat Angels, and the EP Red Planet. And they kept coming back – their most recent appearance being a 2009 sell-out gig at Sheffield's Academy (formerly the Top Rank).

"It was an absolute disaster.
We were abysmal."
Steve Fellows

Photo: Z.Rodak

▲ Comsat Angels

The Extras at The Limit

Photo: Pete Hill

The Extras

Probably the biggest thing on the Sheffield band scene when The Limit opened was The Extras.

Martin Lilleker said: "Theirs is a classic story of a band that should have made it but for the vagaries of the record industry and managing to be in the right place at the right time."

A move to London in 1978 to try their luck proved to be their downfall but no-one, least of all the band, saw it coming. Up until that point they couldn't put a foot wrong.

Extras member Robin Markin said: "Gigs came in right, left and centre. We played with the Boomtown Rats at the university, Siouxsie and the Banshees at the Outlook at Doncaster and Slaughter and the Dogs at the Top Rank. And the entire A&R department from Phonogram Records turned up unannounced to see us play."

They returned from London to do a show in the early days of The Limit in 1978. Mark Albrow said: "The Extras were the only group that I was aware of in Sheffield at the time. Their attitude to the music business was that they were going to get a big record deal. They went to London and came back and did this concert at The Limit. It was really disappointing."

But The Extras - along with The Push - could play as often as they liked as far as Limit management were concerned. Paul Unwin said: "We could guarantee that if The Extras or The Push were playing we'd have a good night."

But he also said they'd got one fatal flaw.

"The Extras did what every band shouldn't do: they became famous before they actually got famous. It cost you a tenner to talk to them and there was a definite attitude."

They did get an offer from Phonogram: a £1,000 advance for a three-singles deal. They turned it down and held out for something better that never materialised.

Theirs was a catalogue of disasters, according to Phil Oakey: "The Extras went to London because they always did the wrong thing. Whatever you shouldn't do, they were doing."

Pulp

Though he played The Limit on many occasions, front man Jarvis Cocker's on-stage debut in a wheelchair was his most legendary.

The way he ended up in that position was pretty impressive as well.

He had cleverly decided to impress a girl with his Spiderman act and managed to fall out of a Division Street first-floor flat window in the process and land on the pavement in front of the Sven Books sex shop.

He ended up in hospital for six weeks with broken ankle, broken wrist and fractured pelvis.

"It was just senseless bravado," he said. "Which is quite out of character. I realised I didn't have the strength to do it, or to climb back in, so I had to count to three and let go."

His month and a half stay in hospital certainly gave him plenty of time to mull over the dos and don'ts of hanging on to window ledges.

The wheelchair gig took place at The Limit on January 14, 1986.

Jarvis Cocker said you knew where you stood with the venue and that he preferred it to The Leadmill, which also hosted numerous Pulp gigs.

"You knew that George Webster was only in it for the money, whereas The Leadmill would always come on with 'we're for the kids, we're community arts, diddly, da diddly do…' and then pay £50."

He had cleverly decided to impress a girl with his Spiderman act and managed to fall out of a Division Street first-floor flat window.

◀ **Pulp** Photo: Pete Hill

Photo: Pete Hill

Artery with future Limit manager Gary Wilson (far right)

Artery

The band that built a relationship with The Limit in more ways than one – their drummer Gary Wilson ended up as the venue's manager.

One particular early gig in 1979 saw local pundit Martin X Russian singing the band's praises despite writing off the venue's free showcase nights for local artists in NMX fanzine.

"Free nights at The Limit have long since ceased to be the much needed showcase for local talent they started out as. Tonight the only Sheffield band on were Artery, who got the duff opening spot... despite a less than perfect sound they came over as a group with stunning originality and commercial potential.

"They did all their favourites – 'Perhaps', 'Turtle', 'Mother Moon', 'Louise', 'The Clown', 'Weak light...' and 'Toytown'. Every song came over powerfully."

Disease

Limit punter Richard Chatterton said: "Local band Disease stepped out from backstage before they were 'on' and asked every member of the audience what their names were, and then incorporated this information into a song, to a throbbing baseline. "Hello Rich, hello Carol, hello Dave, hello Jo, hello Sally, hello Neil..." I thought that was so cool."

Limit co-owner Kevan Johnson decided he'd done his bit for Sheffield music by 1979.

NMX famously quoted him as saying: "We're not having any more local groups on here. They're all rubbish. You can print that."

He wasn't particularly bothered about reviewers either: Martin X Russian was subsequently banned from the venue.

Bands normally faired better when Kevan Johnson was otherwise engaged, by all accounts. Paul Unwin said: "Kevan's knowledge of music could be written on the edge of a pin."

Gary Wilson said: "I went down one night and this band was playing. Kevan Johnson came in, watched them for about ten seconds and said: 'Tell them to fuck off'. This kid had to go on stage and unplug them."

"We're not having any more local groups on here. They're all rubbish. You can print that."

CHAPTER FIVE

Seminal gigs

AND GENERAL **DEBAUCHERY** OF THE EARLY YEARS

There's no doubt that The Limit hosted some of the most legendary and memorable gigs in Sheffield's music history.

Its first couple of years were absolutely relentless in terms of output and quality of artist.

The six-night-a-week Limit gig roster read like a who's who of music from the late seventies/early eighties.

One of the gigs – the UK debut of the B-52s at The Limit on July 24, 1979 – was ranked as one of the best gigs ever in the UK by intellectual rock bible Q Magazine. And if the bands weren't playing they were arriving unannounced as punters – everyone from Pink Floyd to Bay City Rollers stumbled into the place.

"If there's one thing George Webster taught me it was to treat the bands well." Gary Wilson

Much of The Limit's success in booking so many high profile acts and bagging artists who were about to break both nationally and globally was their attitude towards the acts and their road crews.

Gary Wilson: "If there's one thing George Webster taught me it was to treat the bands well."

Selector
Photo:
Pete Hill

The mantra worked like a dream in The Limit and they started making waves nationally and internationally through promoting gigs in bigger venues like Top Rank and Sheffield City Hall and their eventual purchase of Sheffield Lyceum.

They bagged virtually every punk band doing the rounds in the late seventies. The Limit caught the bands as they were either on their ascendancy or just breaking. Acts like Siouxsie and the Banshees, Adam & the Ants, Sham 69, Skids, Dickies, Lurkers, UK Subs, 999, Angelic Upstarts, Cockney Rejects, Generation X, Wayne/Jayne County, Penetration and more.

They bagged virtually every punk band doing the rounds in the late seventies. The Limit caught the bands as they were either on their ascendancy or just breaking.

They absolutely cleaned up on the ska movement which kicked into gear within months of The Limit's inception and they staged groundbreaking debut Sheffield gigs from Specials, Madness, The Beat, Selector, Bad Manners, Modettes and more. American alternative artists like The Cramps and David Johansen (with three quarters of the New York Dolls) made a bee-line for the place.

They had a big part to play in the rise of artists who went on to became part of rock's elite:

U2, The Pretenders, The Tourists (featuring Annie Lennox and Dave Stewart who also returned as Eurythmics), Simple Minds, The Police - all either performed at The Limit or the management promoted them in a larger venue.

Though the venue never embraced rock music massively – that was left to former Limit bouncer Steve Baxendale who opened Rebels rock club at the venue formerly known as Penthouse, once operated by Peter Stringfellow – it did play host to a few existing or future rock monsters like Death Cult (later to become The Cult), Led Zeppelin front man Robert Plant and Sheffield's own Def Leppard.

Soon to be legendary acts like Joy Division and The Shamen played when they were nobodys while, probably more bizarrely, other rock stars like Bay City Rollers and David Cassidy turned up unannounced so they could try and get a drink in peace knowing Limit audiences would have little or no interest in them.

The Limit also promoted a lot of matinee performances for the under-18s, something almost unheard of these days.

Everyone from London punky/Oi merchants Cockney Rejects to Malcolm McLaren hopefuls Bow Wow Wow entertained the younger whippersnappers packed into the venue.

A major nod has to go to one Ged Doughty, who looked after much of the band-booking in the early days.

He'd already made a name for himself at Sheffield Polytechnic and went on to work for Virgin boss Richard Branson in later years.

Despite its live roster becoming a shadow of its former self in later years, The Limit continued to book acts and its early success helped pave the way for venues like Dingwells and The Leadmill which soon set up in direct competition.

The prized Limit For Life Pass that gave free admission... forever

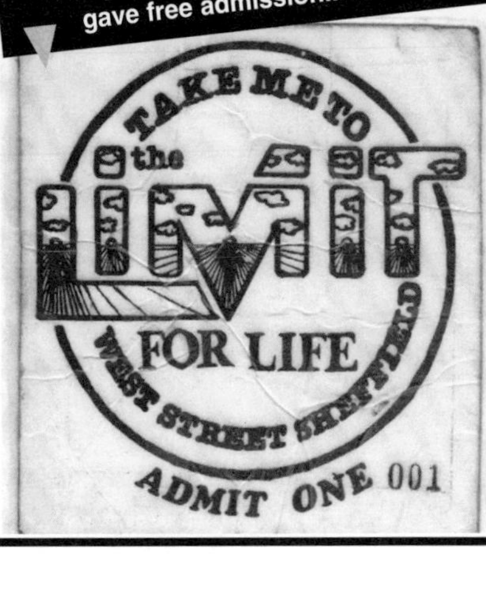

THE HIGHLIGHTS (AND A FEW LOWLIGHTS)

B-52s

The July 24, 1979 show of the B-52s was ranked as one of the seminal gigs of all time in the UK. It was a massive coup to land them. The band's debut in London a few days later attracted everyone from Limit favourite Joe Jackson to Scritti Politti in the audience. Not surprising then that half of Sheffield claimed to be at The Limit that night. It was the band's UK debut and the buzz around the city was phenomenal in the days leading up to the event.

The club was already over a year into its stride but this gig was a massive milestone, even by Limit standards.

The venue was absolutely heaving and that was before the trademark beehive hairstyles of Kate Pierson and Cindy Wilson came on stage.

Their 'Rock Lobster' single, which became one of the most requested tracks in the history of The Limit, was already making massive waves across the UK.

Richard Malik: "I'd never seen anything like the B-52s in my life before and it made a real impact on the audience that night. The styles were more outlandish than normal and there were definitely a few attempts at beehives resembling the girls in the band. The Limit was better known for punk bands at that point and the B-52s' blend of dance and surf music introduced a whole new audience to the place.

"I remember they must have played most of their first album, with tracks like 'Planet Claire' and 'Downtown' really standing out. But it was the massive 'Rock Lobster' that really brought the house down. I remember it was such an addictive tune – it was in my head for days after!"

The Cramps

Cramps front man Lux Interior made probably the most unceremonious exit of any star from the stage of The Limit.

They were nearing the height of their popularity when they performed in the early years of the club, a factor which didn't make a blind bit of difference to club co-owner Kevan Johnson.

Martin Bellamy said: "The Limit ceiling – which was a kind of polystyrene material - was low anyway and with a couple-of-feet-high stage it was even lower.

"Anyway, Cramps front man Lux Interior discovered the ceiling would come down like snow if it was pushed and proceeded to have a field day with it.

"Limit co-owner Kevan Johnson looked on in absolute disgust and said 'there's no way he's doing an encore'.

"Ex-butcher turned Limit doorman Chris Baker was on duty that night and he was tasked with doing the honours.

"Chris jumped on stage, grabbed the singer by his arse and collar and launched him straight back off the stage and through the dressing-room door.

"It was even funnier because the NME were in the club doing a review that night and they said something along the lines of 'the audience were denied an encore because the resident host decided Lux Interior was far better off in the dressing-room'."

The Cramps

Joy Division

The Ian Curtis phenomenon, still in its infancy at that point, arrived at The Limit as part of a Factory Records package in the early months of the club. His fledgling Joy Division were sandwiched between A Certain Ratio and Orchestral Manoeuvres in the Dark.

Martin X Russian of NMX fanzine was hardly enthused: "I think it's wrong to categorise but there are certain bands you just can't help lumping together and two of them are A Certain Ratio and Joy Division.

"What was most disturbing was that they all looked exactly the same: fresh-faced young intellectuals in grey straight-leg trousers and dull coloured open neck shirts.

"The Manchester look. Afterwards in the dressing room I found it impossible to decide who was in which band – very embarrassing. Both the image and the music are very much orientated towards Wire/early Subway Sect.

"Grey/bleak/cold/emotionless. It may not convey much and they're all words which have been used before but they really are the most appropriate adjectives.

"A Certain Ratio were on first, in front of a sparse and largely apathetic audience. Their songs were very repetitive and though it wasn't a long set it seemed like it was. The sound was quite original, with the unlikely presence of a black jazz-rock drummer behind a massive kit and speedy bass lines dominating the mix.

"On top of that the two guitarists seemed to be competing to see who could get the most annoying high pitched noises out of their instruments.

"The singer warbled in a bass drone well out of tune with the music. The overall effect was compelling for the first couple of numbers but afterwards got slightly tedious, only picking up for the storming finale of 'Genotype' in which the music slowly degenerated for a climax of pure noise."

"The singer warbled in a bass drone well out of tune with the music. The overall effect was compelling for the first couple of numbers but afterwards got slightly tedious."

"JOY DIVISION were slightly more palatable to the average punter largely because of a more conventional guitar sound. They even had guitar solos! Most of the music was fast and moderately danceable, best of the night, almost punk. Main feature of their stage presence was their singer, who has developed a highly original way of waving his arms about, best described as the 'hand pogo' (punk version of the hand jive). He also leapt about a lot, jumped into the audience and fell over. God knows what he'd been taking but I'm sure he wouldn't do it if he knew what a prat he looked. Full marks for effort anyway.

"By the time Orchestral Manoeuvres came on The Limit was fast emptying. I'd seen them before in Manchester and my opinion hasn't changed. They're an electronic duo consisting of a keyboards player and a singer who occasionally plays bass or other keyboards. Undoubtedly the star of the group is a tape recorder, which does the rhythm track, bass lines and, on one song, saxophone. It makes you wonder why they have bothered coming on stage at all. The music is blatant Human League-isms, except this lot only have one good tune (the single 'Electricity') and no original ideas.

"Fortunately Orchestral Manoeuvres prefabricated boredom didn't eclipse the good points of the other two bands and it's good to see The Limit still occasionally putting on worthwhile gigs."

Unfortunately, principles stopped two locals dining out on this legendary Sheffield Joy Division appearance for the rest of their days.

Clive Porter: "I know we did not see Joy Division. My memory is that they were charging £1.25 and my friend Chris and I thought that was too much for a relatively unknown band. Sadly, Ian Curtis died not long after... I have long since regretted that bit of tight fistedness. At the time we probably claimed it was a matter of principle."

U2

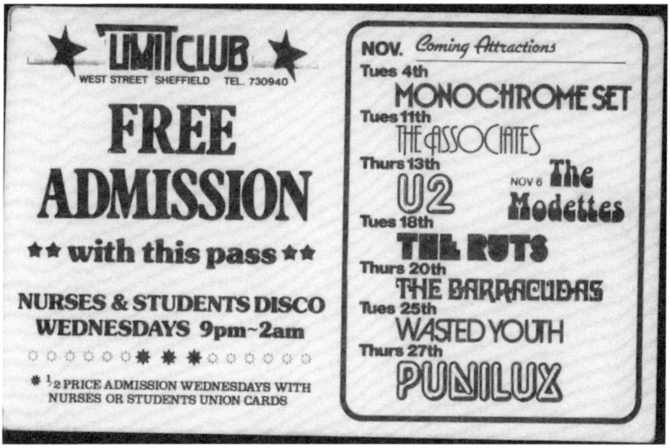

Though it was one of the lowest turn-outs in the history of The Limit, U2 definitely played as though they meant it according to George Webster:

"I had a white label copy of their album and I loved it. I got a call from Wasted Talent who said they were struggling to get them gigs. I said 'we'll put them on in here'. They were fabulous but only 14 customers turned up.

"They played as though they were performing at Shea Stadium."

Klive Humberstone of Sheffield band In The Nursery said an accident involving Bono's trousers was his residing memory: "Bono reached up to touch the ceiling and his leather pants split.

"I tried to enjoy them, to feel part of it, but the execution of the songs just didn't work, no tension, nothing held back. No structure or mystery. Bono is great though - a searching stare - drawing you in - acknowledging your presence. He's great at singing - soulful and meaningful - but the music was too complete, too polished. Difficult to explain in words."

The Undertones

Northern Ireland's finest, The Undertones were the only band in The Limit management's history to request 'fish and chips' on their rider.

Thankfully club management could happily ply them with enough to sink a North Sea ferry, they'd got a chippy bang next door on West Street.

The Undertones, who were just breaking into the big time when they performed at the West Street venue, were at their pop/punk finest by all accounts.

Steven Bliwert, who travelled down from Teeside for the gig, said: "I'd heard Teenage Kicks on John Peel, I think it was, and it totally blew me away. I thought I've got to see this band and ended up travelling down from Middlesbrough with my mates. I've never seen a front man put so much effort into it as Fergal Sharkey did that night. I remember pogoing down the front for England and rushing out to buy their debut album as soon as it hit the shops. What a gig. I think we were all singing Teenage Kicks in the van back up to Teeside.

"We used to have regular trips to The Limit – nobody was doing what they were doing around our way".

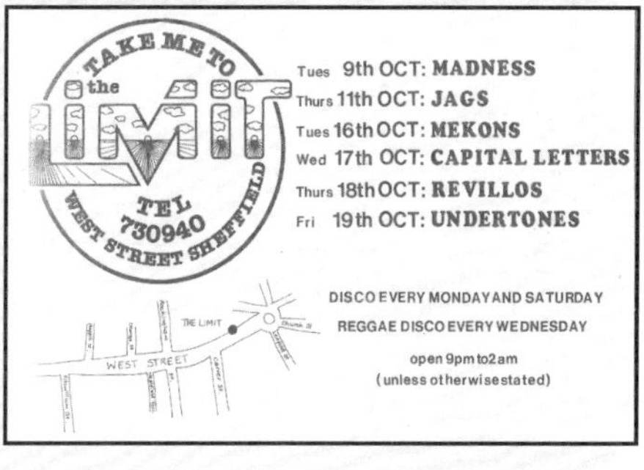

Robert Plant at The Limit
Photo: Andy Smith

Robert Plant/The Honeydrippers

Few Limit gigs have caused as much of a stir as when Led Zeppelin front man Robert Plant turned up to do a bit of a soiree with his former band, The Honeydrippers. In fact the queue stretched up West Street and beyond...

Karen Davies said: "Nobody could quite believe such a legend could be performing in a place like The Limit, the anticipation was out of this world. The queue was so long we were debating whether to bother at all. We knew the club was only a small capacity and our hearts sank with every group they let in. And then, as we were nearly through the door, security said they were full and we might as well go home. We were absolutely gutted – we must have been in that queue for nearly two hours.

"But then, and we still can't believe it to this day, a group of five people left the club without saying a word and we were let in.

"I still rank it as one of the best gigs I've ever been to. Where else could you go to be within inches of Robert Plant!"

Limit manager Kevan Johnson was even nearer.

"I was drinking champagne with Robert Plant in the kitchen. He was a great bloke."

Generation X

Martin Bellamy: "I ended up being Billy Idol's bodyguard for the night. He was absolutely petrified and was hanging on to the back of my shirt for dear life. I had to escort him through the crowd with all these people thrusting magazines and photos for signing. I don't know why he was so scared – they were his fans!"

Limit head of security that night Ivan Bradley said it was one of the best gigs he'd ever seen. The vinyl wasn't quite so exciting.

"Generation X were one of the best live experiences I'd ever seen. I ended up going out to buy two of their albums after the show – unfortunately they were shit."

Joe Jackson and Skids

Attempts at encores didn't always bite the dust in such unconventional style as The Cramps. In fact two particular acts were happy (and allowed) to play most of the night.

Burton-on-Trent born new wave artist Joe Jackson – a bit of a Limit favourite by all accounts - probably holds the record for the most encores at The Limit: he did seven, according to Martin Bellamy.

At least he had enough material to keep things fresh, which was a far cry from Skids, who pop up for second place with six encores.

"They ended up having to do 'Into The Valley' again as they'd run out of ideas," says Bellamy.

But it didn't stop the place going mad, with front man Richard Jobson's trademark high-kicking dance that is still giving out hernias to this day.

Early Limit-goer Jon Downing said:
"The place was just wild with that weird dance."

Squeeze

Martin Bellamy: "Their gear was held up in Ireland from a gig they'd played there the night before. It finally arrived at 9pm and various members of the queue outside were conscripted to help carry everything into the club."

Bow Wow Wow

Tony Beesley:
"December 1980; I was still a 15-year-old Punk Rocker and had seen many great (and a few not so great) gigs in Sheffield, mostly at the Top Rank. Following an earlier attempt to get into The Limit that had failed miserably, I heard that the post-Adam & the Ants/Malcolm McLaren put-together group 'Bow Wow Wow' were doing an afternoon show for us young uns at The Limit club. Ok let's check them out I thought!

"Annabella came on followed by the rest of the group. I may be wrong but I think they were dressed pirate-influenced style... not in an Adam Ant style but more of an authentic creative look.

"Time may erode the exact details but that's how I recall the image: robes, belts and buckles and the only item that may have ruined the pirate look... the pirate hat that Annabella had on. I mean, how many pirates would go for the Caribbean 'Kiss me Quick' look? I could be wrong about these details...I don't know for sure.

"The songs they played were all very energetic. I was struck by the new sound that was very different to all of the other groups I had been to see and, yes, there was a kind of similarity to the Adam & the Ants sound but these songs sounded less formulated.

"Annabella seemed nervous but put on a good show. I was stood straight in front of her as she bellowed out the songs. She was the same age as me and I remember being very impressed by her energy and commitment to putting on a good set. Almost as much energy that me and my mates showed at our regular youth club pogo sessions.

Jools Holland at The Limit

"The punks there were dancing at the front all around where I was stood but it was nothing like being rammed up against the Top Rank stage and getting trapped between a pogoing mass and the stage.

"The show was short and sweet, probably only half an hour I would say.

"They played 'C-30, C-60, C-90 GO' at least twice, maybe three times. I know they ran out of songs and repeated two or three of them.

"They did an encore which went down well and I believe possibly another encore. I reckon they made a great debut in Sheffield and not long afterwards I bought their cassette-only release 'Cassette Pet', which was a kind of mini-album and was probably as long as their set itself."

Punishment of Luxury and Vice Versa

NMX scribe Gary Birchall said:
"Punishment of Luxury got an encore for their gig, deservedly so after a consistent and captivating set. The focal point is singer Brian Bond, who said he looked like Peter Gabriel with a heavier backing. In fact he has similarities to the old time Gabriel and that's no bad thing.

"The music was original enough to keep it out of the heavy metal zone, often quite innovative. The other essential factor was the band's choreography – impressive and devo-esque, though not close enough to be called a rip-off.

"The fun of it all did grate a little when for the encore they repeated their opening number, the single 'Puppet Life', complete with identical dance routine, which seemed rather silly and superficial. It was still a great set."

"Punishment of Luxury were an odd act, like a progressive rock punk band, influenced by Peter Gabriel's stage antics as much as those of Johnny Rotten. Their 'Puppet Life ' anthem became one of the most heard sounds on The Limit dance floor."

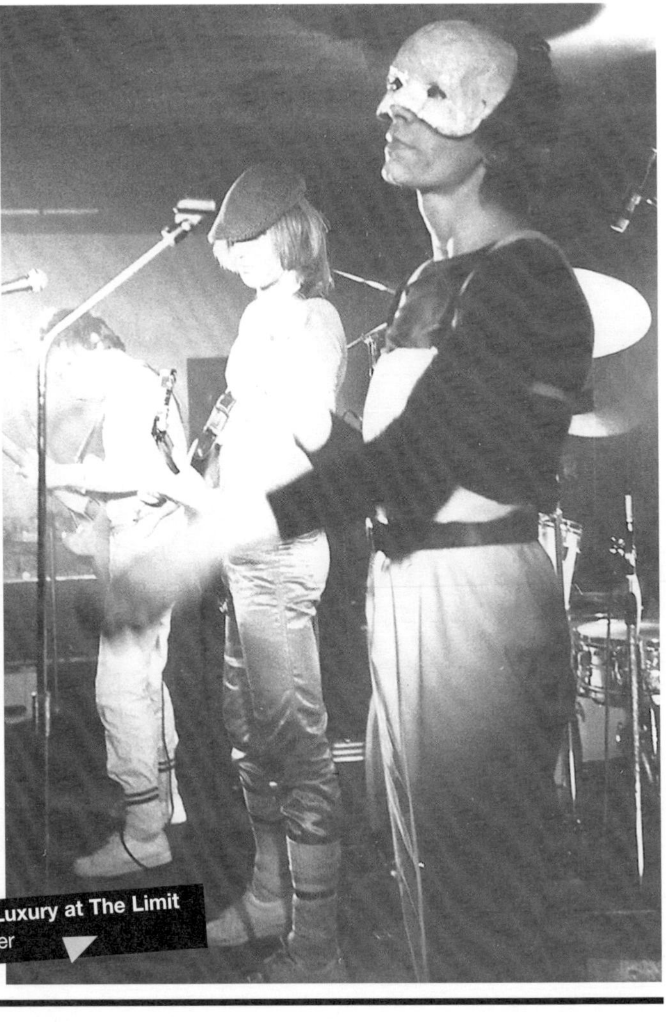

Punishment of Luxury at The Limit
Photo Clive Porter

Vice Versa Photo: Pete Hill

"Support were Vice Versa. First time I saw this band, in October 1978, they were interesting; second time round they dragged and this time they were awful. Initially there was polite applause but after two songs the audience were too bored to pull their hands from their pockets. Vice Versa's pretension ranges from the predictably trendy communication with the audience to their embarrassing attempts to be inaccessible and cold. To be successfully weird you've got to smile a bit, but that would spoil the pose, wouldn't it?"

It's fair to say Vice Versa (when they became ABC) had the last laugh.

Limit regular Richard Chatterton:

"Punishment of Luxury were an odd act, like a progressive rock punk band, influenced by Peter Gabriel's stage antics as much as those of Johnny Rotten. Their 'Puppet Life ' anthem became one of the most heard sounds on the Limit dance floor, with it's opening 'Sister Suzie' shout.

They had long hair, wore white make-up and effected a puppet-like dance on one of the tracks, although when I was leaving someone told me that they had toned much of the theatrics down."

Vice Versa with the addition of Martin Fry before they went on to become ABC Photo: Pete Hill

Rockabilly rebels at The Limit Photo: Chris Waker

The Jags

John Quinn, journalist with The Star, said: "I remember when The Jags played The Limit. My mum worked in a hotel at the time and told me that there was a band staying there, The Jam. I thought of all the money I could make selling their autographs to our school's mod contingent so asked her to get me them. She came back from work and gave me the autographs of a group of people I'd never heard of in my life. Back Of My Hand was a good single though."

Teardrop Explodes

This band probably didn't benefit too much from their review in NMX fanzine. The mag's owner was still banned and Teardrop Explodes didn't get a mention until the last line of the review. Makes for good reading, all the same.

"MXR [Martin X Russian] ought to be allowed in this place, the ridiculous banning only satisfies George Webster's vanity after all. Perhaps he should moor a giant inflatable balloon-face of himself to The Limit sign, to hitch yobbos to if they cause trouble. The Khomeni Webster – a new land-mark, pilgrimages of Brian Ferry looka-likes from the Blue Bell, via The Stonehouse. More would be achieved by letting MXR in again, the Voice of Reason speaks out etc, not that any-one's listening these days. The Limit never seems to change at all, except that the drinks are now relatively cheap since pub prices are high now. I always enjoy myself when I go down, the atmosphere suits inebriation far more than music.

"The audience was fairly small, less than at their recent Nowsoc gig, the lawnmowers roar outside my window, so I'll keep it short – Teardrops have a few great pop songs and lots of near misses, a rich powerful sound, nice looks, good back up, and could be quite famous. GPD."

The Macc Lads

While the middle of the eighties was disap-pearing up its own arse in a haze of animal rights, women's rights and all round pc-charged Armageddon, one band triumphed in the face of adversity and saved the nation.

The Macc Lads were the crudest, rudest piss-take in the history of rock'n'roll up until that point.

They attracted a pretty frightening audience of 50% punk rocker, 50% football hooligan, all fired up on 110% lager.

Macc Lads gigs at The Limit were a truly-mental experience.

Richard Malik said: "When The Macc Lads first caught on it was just the punks turning up. The later shows were total carnage – it was just a hooligan-fest.

"The next time I'd see half the audience they'd be fighting at SUFC or SWFC football matches."

Martin Bellamy said: "When The Macc Lads used to come down, the club would be absolutely rammed – you were just pushed against the back wall. Their nights were great – it was just a politically incorrect laugh."

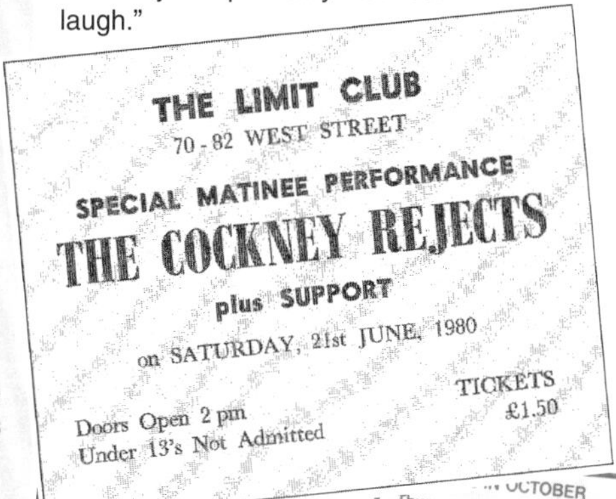

The Photos at The Limit Photo: Pete Hill

The Photos

Tony Beesley: "Me and a mate went to see the Photos at The Limit club. I think it was a Thursday night during the early Summer of 1981. I had their LP and a few singles and, although not my favourite band of the time, I felt that they were very under-rated, especially the image that the music press were giving them, 'the poor man's Blondie'. So the chance of going to see them play live was something I was quite looking forward to. I kind of figured that they would be good, but not as good as they were on the night.

"Like many gigs from the punk and post-punk era that I attended, lots of them are now very hazy memories, some have even been almost completely forgotten and more than a few I am told by friends that we went along to I have no recollections of at all. Thankfully, there are some great memories still floating about in the old memory bank. What can I remember of the Photos at The Limit club? Well, without wanting to sound too shallow (I was a hormone-driven teenager remember and yes we punks did have a sex drive too) the most abiding image I have of that night is of singer Wendy Wu stood centre stage, lips almost kissing the mike, fish-net stockings and black leather mini skirt, with long dark flowing hair and looking the sexiest woman I had ever seen. Her voice sublime as she sang the words to 'Irene', 'Do You have Fun' and 'Barbarellas' amongst most of their first and only LP tracks (their cancelled follow-up finally saw the light of day on CD a couple of years ago). The band were tight as hell and were in complete control of the tempo and pace of the songs all throughout the set. I don't remember them being a group that moved around that much (I may be wrong - it could have been my transfixation on Wendy Wu) but they had a very together sound and delivered their songs in a really accomplished way, unlike most other punk bands I had seen. I suppose their songs were very much pop songs with a punky power pop drive and they had been around for quite a while by that point (first as Satans Rats in 1977 minus Wendy Wu) so they were great musicians too.

"The Photos' set that night was one of the very best I saw that year and possibly in amongst the top end of my favourite-ever gigs. The club itself was only about less than half full. We had a couple of pints of the much maligned Limit lager but we didn't complain, we were underage anyway. I think they were on-stage around the 1am mark or maybe earlier. I know we seemed to be in the club for quite some time before they hit the stage. Even so, they were well worth the wait and after the gig me and my mate wandered into the city centre looking for any taxis left hanging around. I don't know if we walked the whole 12 miles or so home as we sometimes did. I do know that The Photos at The Limit club far exceeded my expectations. The next day the first record on my record player was the 'Irene' e.p."

"Like many gigs from the punk and post-punk era that I attended, lots of them are now very hazy memories, some have even been almost completely forgotten and more than a few I am told by friends that we went along to I have no recollections of at all."
Tony Beesley

Q Tips at The Limit Photo: Pete Hill

TAKE ME TO the LIMIT
TEL 730940
WEST STREET SHEFFIELD

Thursday November 30th
WILD HORSES
with Brian Robertson & Jimmy Bain

Friday December 1st
STRAIGHTS
(All Girl New Wave Band)

Tuesday December 5th
THE MEKONS

Wednesday December 6th
Reggae with
CAPITAL LETTERS

Thursday December 7th
CAFE JACQUES

Friday December 8th
THE ADVERTS

Students Free Monday, Discount Tuesday and Wednesday

Open 9 pm-2 am

TAKE ME TO the LIMIT
TEL 730940
WEST STREET SHEFFIELD

Thursday 16th
Eric Bell Band (formally of Thin Lizzy)

Friday 17th
Blitz Krieg Bop

Saturday 18th
Disco with Paul Unwin

Monday 20th
Free Students Disco

All students & nurses with card, free admission.

Tuesday 21st
Jazz Rock with 64 Spoons

Wednesday 22nd
Reggae Band Tribesman

Mon-Wed
Students Discount with card

TAKE ME TO the LIMIT
TEL 730940
WEST STREET SHEFFIELD

Thursday, November 23rd
From U.S.A.
DAVID JOHANSEN
(ex New York Dolls)
N.B: Doors open 8 pm Tonight

Friday, November 24th
SORE THROAT

Tuesday, November 28th
POLICE

Wednesday, November 29th
Reggae with
IMMIGRANT

Students Free Monday, Discount Tuesday and Wednesday

Open 9 pm-2 am

Terry & Jerry at The Limit Photo: Tracy Pidd

TV Smith's Explorers

Tony Beesley: "I loved the Adverts. Had every one of their records, read all of their interviews in the music weeklies, had a big thing for Gaye Advert and even had their name painted on the back of an old Denim jacket of mine in white model paint. Some of my mates saw them at The Limit club and the Top Rank (one of my very best mates John Harrsion got thrown on to the stage right at Gaye Advert's feet) as well as Doncaster Outlook club and Rotherham Windmill club but poor old me never even got a glimpse of 'em live. Life is full of regrets eh?

"Not long after the Adverts split, singer TV Smith reappeared back on the scene. My first knowledge of him was the 'Tomahawk cruise' 45 which was a superb debut single, in January of '81. Then while on a trip to Manchester Mayflower club a couple of months later, I bought the 'Grinding Halt' fanzine which had a fantastic interview with TV Smith in. Yes TV Smith was back on the scene and I was more than eager to make up for missing The Adverts.

"Summer 1981 and I pestered my mate Andy Morton to come along and see TV and his new band, The Explorers, at The Limit. I think it pissed it down that night as we ventured up West Street and into the club. First off, we had a couple of pints and got to grips with our surroundings. There were a few familiar faces in there but not really anyone we knew to speak to. We kept ourselves to ourselves as we soaked up the post-punk tunes being spun by the DJ and felt the onset of under-age drinking flow into our bloodstreams. There was a rougher edge to hanging out in The Limit club than the typical punk venues of the day. I always sensed the feeling that violence could easily kick off at any time. Nothing major ever happened while I was in the place but, after one of the handful of gigs I went to there, I came out with a knife incision in the back of my leather jacket. Whether it was this night, I have no idea. I had felt something as the small crowd surged forward but never thought much about it. I think there were some quite seedy fellas behind us but I was young and didn't give it much serious thought. Anyway, apart from that foreboding atmosphere, which really wasn't that unusual to feel back in those days, all was fine. Not long before the band came on stage, some guys were shouting out 'Gary Gilmores eyes'. I knew that there was no chance of that getting played and rightly so. Hadn't The Adverts split up after all?

"Images of the actual set are splintered after all these years. The set consisted of the whole 'Last words of the Great Explorer' LP and the couple of single B-sides, like one of my particular faves, 'Looking down on London'.

"TV Smith was full of energy that night. He was wearing his classic shirt and tie, looking not that dissimilar to the image of classic Adverts days."
Tony Beesley

"TV Smith was full of energy that night. He was wearing his classic shirt and tie, looking not that dissimilar to the image of classic Adverts days. The songs could well have been an extension of Adverts material, which I suppose they were really, with an extra maturity and musical proficiency. TV came into the audience at some points singing along and exuberantly giving it his best. The musicians in the Explorers were as good as if not better than most I had seen play live up until that point. To me at the time, this was what post-punk music should have been aspiring to.

"Unfortunately, the Explorers songs were too accomplished to appeal to the hardcore punk crowd and too punk-orientated to cross over that far into the ears of the more discerning music lover. Like many talented groups around at that time, TV Smith's Explorers were almost ignored and subsequently lost within the confused and directionless climate of the punk fall-out. It is only now and during more recent years that the real talents of songwriters such as TV Smith have truly shone through into the hearts of an older and much wiser punk generation."

"The Limit club was red hot that night even though it was pissing it down outside. The gig, for me personally, was a great one and I remember looking forward to getting the chance to see TV Smith's Explorers again at some point. Following the gig, me and Andy - who comments to this day that he is glad I managed to persuade him to go the gig - set off on our travels home to good old Rawmarsh. I don't recall the journey home but I can clearly remember turning the corner of my street at around 2 or 3am and seeing my poor old mother sat on our front wall. She had come home at 12ish to discover that I had taken both house keys with me to The Limit and she had been locked out of the house. It must have stopped raining before then, otherwise she would have killed me. Instead I got the bollocking that I deserved but it was worth it."

Gong

Though The Limit was used to some pretty weird and wonderful sights via the bands, their entourages and the behaviour of the punters, there was nothing that could have prepared the place for the arrival of Gong, led by celebrated guitarist Steve Hillage.

Paul Unwin: "I was outside the door of the club and all I could hear was 'baaing' noises and the sounds of hens clucking.

I went inside and there's two goats behind the bar and goat crap everywhere. There are about four hens and two chickens in a box.

"Vernon [Price] had been left to look after the band and I said 'where's the tour manager?' and he said 'I don't know'. I said 'why have I employed you to let them bring goats in here?'

"Vernon obviously didn't see it as out of the ordinary to have livestock in nightclubs in the late seventies. He said: 'Well they can't leave them on the bus can they?'"

The menagerie returned to the coach to be replaced by the Gong following, who didn't sound that dissimilar to the animals.

Paul Unwin: "When the crowd came in they looked as though they'd been swept in from 1972. As soon as the band came on they sat cross-legged on the floor and I'm thinking 'this place is meant to be Sheffield's ultimate punk club'!"

"I went inside and there's two goats behind the bar and goat crap everywhere. There are about four hens and two chickens in a box." Paul Unwin

Bill Nelson (ex. Be Bop Deluxe)

Jon Downing: "The gig was absolutely superb – it was packed solid. I remember some bloke in the crowd shouting 'Big Bill' through the entire gig."

Clare Grogan of Altered Images at The Limit

Echo and the Bunnymen
Photo: Pete Hill

Lords of the New Church

Tony Beesley said: "1982 and punk rock was as dead as doornails for me. I couldn't stand the nihilism and apathy of the new punk bands who were banging away aimlessly at their instruments at the time. If 1981 had seen the very first signs that punk was swiftly becoming a musical bore and as rule-book-orientated as any of the boring old farts it was meant to kick aside, then 1982 was as boring as 1975, before punk had even really started. There was positive punk (ok in concept and ideals and a genuine stab at turning the next corner but ultimately a mere proto-type for Goth etc); the old stalwarts such as The Damned were writing and performing with one foot in the punk scene and the other more comfortably treading water with their love of pre-punk prog rock; and post-punk fuelled psychedelia. Lydon had abandoned all original PIL concepts and was well on his way to being the Celebrity we all know in the modern day.

The Clash now firmly had their sights blinkered with all of the pitfalls of major rock stardom and would soon suffer the consequences of loving the USA just that bit too much and The Jam, although admirably still loyal to their real fans and the punk ideals, were slowly being cornered into a mainstream of pop star adulation. When Weller called it a day towards the end of the year, strange as this might seem coming from a massive Jam fan, it was almost a breath of fresh air. If punk was failing from its original pioneers and its most ardent punk fans and their new punk attempts, why not form a new punk supergroup to kick things back into style. Lords of the New Church came from the ashes of The Damned, Dead Boys, Sham 69 and the Barracudas and, while I am sure they most likely did not consciously seriously think about the punk supergroup tag being that relevant, they did not exactly play it down that much. Nevertheless, expectations were high.

"Me and my mate Clarkey were quite excited about going to see the Lords of the new Church at that old church of punk gospel, The Limit club. I had bought the self-titled debut single and he had even got me to paint the cover of their just-released first album on the back of his leather jacket. This gig... I can clearly recall how we got there and how we got back, what a rarity. My brother drove us up, dropped us off and later on picked us up after we rang him from the nearest phone box.

"The thing that most impressed me about these punk leftovers was the talent of Brian James and his clear love of the sound of garage rock, Stooges, New York Dolls and the sound of metal clashing with glam and punk rock. His songs were all written in this vein and the whole image of Brian James was one of the long tradition of Stones, Stooges, Dolls through punk and onwards through rock n' roll visuals and live experience. Here was genuine punk (in the sixties sense of the term) and these guys were the only exponents at the time to keep that flame burning. It's a pity they swiftly became just as boring as all the rest of the struggling punk gang of the early '80s.

John Cooper-Clarke at The Limit

"However, tonight the four-piece of former Dead Boy and future rock fatality singer Stiv Bators, ex Sham bass player Dave Treggena, ex Barracuda punk surfer Nick Turner on drums and Damned immortal Brian James on guitar really set the stage of The Limit club alight with pure rock'n'roll energy. The band played three-quarters of an hour or so of fantastic blazing rock'n'roll, James giving it every punk guitar hero pose that he could possibly muster and Stiv Bators showing he actually did have the makings of a front man, no matter how forced he had been in USA punk/metal pretenders the Dead Boys. The Limit crowd lapped em up, there were even some signs of almost manic pogoing going on. No shouts for 'New Rose', 'Sonic Reducer' or 'Neat, Neat, Neat' (not that I heard anyway) 'New Church', ' Open your Eyes' and all of the LP passed by in a haze of steaming energetic garage rock. Though, if old solo 45 of Brian James' 'Ain't that a shame' had been performed I would have been well chuffed; I love that song as much as anything James has written post 1977 Damned. If Iggy Pop had been in the crowd he would have leapt up on to the tiny Limit stage to join in the fun. This was quite a special night. I could see the future of rock'n'roll right there in front of me. The trouble was, for me anyhow, the feeling would only last for this very one night. Lords of the New Church 1982 were very briefly something very promising. That night at The Limit club they played to the very best of their abilities. Soon after at the Leadmill, they would play a good but, compared to this night, rather treadmill set. Their Limit club set, which was basically the first LP, was spot on. Can't fault it and, it seemed at the time, enjoyed by almost all of those present - a mix of Limit regulars, disgruntled punks and metal fans. The next day when we played the vinyl representation of the previous night's set I realised how dull the Lords of the New Church sounded on record as opposed to seeing and hearing live. I did buy a couple of their singles after that but soon sold them and consigned the group to bought-and-sold vinyl history. But, that night in mid 1982 the Limit club stage shone bright with the sounds of this new so-called punk supergroup. Maybe we expected too much of our musicians back then. Though when those expectations were met, it was pure bliss!"

Bill Nelson signs autographs at The Limit

Cockney Rejects matinee

Richard Chatterton: "I went along to the afternoon performance by the Cockney Rejects with my two brothers. The concert was for 13-year-olds and upwards but we managed to get 11-year-old Craig, my youngest brother, in and he looked the part in his dog-collar and ripped blazer. I can remember he sat on the floor oozing up the no future vibe! My brothers were later to form Rotherham legends in their own lunchtime, Phil Murray & the Boys from Bury, a bluesy-punk band who are still going to this day."

David Johansen Band

Phil Staniland said: "The main thing I remember about the David Johansen gig is that I got in for nothing, which was quite amazing considering it was a double sell-out. What I mean by that is that the show had sold out so quickly and there had been such a demand for tickets that David J agreed to do two shows on the same night.

"Anyway I remember wandering down the infamous Limit staircase where many a drunk had taken a dive and my appearance at the time was very much in need of repair. I can only think The Limit door people thought I was with the band with my total mopped-up and out-of-control Johnny Thunders hair (which incidentally is now 'in-growing'). I also wore patched-up jeans - not dissimilar to Neil Young's pictured on the 'After the Goldrush' album - and the filthiest Afghan coat imaginable. That's because it had been in the Fargate fountain a few times with me wearing it after many a boozy night in my student days. So basically I was left to wander in for free and no questions were asked.

"As soon as I walked in I bumped into two of my lifelong friends, Andy Parr and Mark Johnson, who I had not arranged to meet there, they were just there because of the importance of the event.

"The band line-up consisted of those who played on David's first and simply titled first solo album, 'David Johansen'. Fellow-Doll Syl Sylvain was playing in the band as well and he handed me his plectrum at the end which I treasured for years until it ended up being lost forever in a farmer's field out in Midhopestones. Another thing I remember is that it was the loudest gig ever. The band were playing some big venues on the tour and their rig was massive. Instead of scaling it down for the venue they used it as it was and I thought they were gonna blow The Limit up with it – it was frightening. I was deaf for about three days afterwards. Anyway you could hardly move in the venue they had let that many people in and at some stage I was

Limit regular Richard Chatterton

Holly and The Italians
Photo: Pete Hill

"I remember there was this sudden violent surge forward and I ended up on my back on the stage."

down at the front, wedged between the small stage and the audience. Incidentally they were playing on the small stage at the side of the DJ box and not the back wall where the stage was moved to in later years. I remember there was this sudden violent surge forward and I ended up on my back on the stage and somehow under David J's feet nearly knocking him over. It caused him to laugh while he was singing above me and he was swaying about trying to kindly avoid my lifeless frame that remained on the stage completely whammoed.

"All of a sudden the infamous black bouncer who was on the door every single night (it seemed) of The Limit's existence clambered on stage picked me up and slung me back into the audience looking like a rag doll as I flew through the air (literally).

"I don't remember much after that apart from the band doing Personality Crisis as an encore and me staggering out on to West Street to face the massive second queue of people going right down the street.

"The majority of the stuff they played that night came from that first album. Classics such as 'Funky but Chic' which I'm certain Duran Duran stole in order to write 'Girls on Film' - just listen to the verses side by side and bear in mind which came first. Also a rendition of the tortured 'Frenchette' and powerhouse versions of 'Girls', and 'Cool Metro' etc. etc. also chucking in the Dolls' classic, 'Looking for a Kiss'.

"It was a historic night for The Limit and for Sheffield because I can't remember ever hearing a story that the Dolls had ever played our fair city and I suppose this was the nearest we ever got."

The Meteors

John Robb: "I remember seeing The Meteors at The Limit and there was a tear gas incident."
Gary Wilson said: "Somebody said something and they went off and came back with machetes, baseball bats and all sorts.

"We had to call the police."

Fad Gadget and the arrival of the new romantics

Richard Chatterton: "Fad Gadget - an electronic band fronted by Frank Tovey. He was holding a pose on stage when some guy behind me shouted: 'Poseur!'. I was standing right at the front (the venue wasn't even half full anyway) and Tovey, holding some kind of cardboard roll, held it over the heckler's head. The guy was wearing a polka-dot top, braces and stripey trousers. 'This guy,' Povey uttered, 'has the cheek to call ME a poseur and just look at him'.

"The guy, now visibly shaken, answered: 'Er...no...I said that you were in a pose as opposed to being a poseur'. Ah, post punk banter.

"The decorative garb of said heckler was proof of a new phenomenon creeping into The Limit. The New Romantic look of the Early Eighties. I was standing at The Limit bar one night, waiting for it to fill up, chatting with a couple of skinheads. We were watching a circle of frilly-white-shirted youths poncing and parading around. One of the skinheads said to me: 'Look at them, like a load of pansy pirates. What's wrong with braces, Doc Martens and a Fred Perry?' Thankfully this movement was short-lived. One of the group, Simon Singleton, was the brother of Steven, who was sax player with the Sheffield group ABC, soon to make a name for themselves nationwide."

"Look at them, like a load of pansy pirates. What's wrong with braces, Doc Martens and a Fred Perry?"

Ska arrives at The Limit

Though The Limit missed out on the start of the punk scene it was ideally placed for the ska explosion of the late '70s.
Specials, Madness, The Beat, Selector and Bad Manners all played legendary gigs as they were just breaking into the big time.
Mark Openshaw said: "I went to all the early ska gigs at The Limit – they were absolutely nuts. We all knew they were part of something special, there was such a buzz going around."

Paul Thompson made his Limit debut at the early ska gigs. He said: "I've never been to gigs that were that busy – there were hundreds and hundreds crammed into that club, god knows what the fire brigade would have said if they'd walked in. We were literally falling on to the stage or actually dancing on it with the bands themselves.

"I remember I wanted to go to the toilet and couldn't move. I just had to hold it in until the gig had finished.

"The Specials were definitely my favourite of all those nights. I can't remember if they'd been on or were just about to go on Top Of The Pops with their Gangsters debut but the place just went absolutely mad when that came on. Front man Terry Hall was just so cool.

"Pork pie hats were just starting to be in vogue – mine bit the dust that night and the back of my parka got ripped. It was worth it all the same. Fantastic times that will never be repeated."

Barbara Fenton meets Level 42's Mark King at their Limit show

First timers and other anecdotes...

Tony Beesley: "I first came across the Limit club by sight whilst on a trip in 1978 to Sheffield with my older brother. We went up West Street and as we were passing the club he pointed over and told me that 'there is one of the clubs where all of your kind of groups play at'. I glanced over the other side of the road and saw a Dickies poster at the side of a doorway. I had heard vaguely of the Dickies but wasn't familiar with any of their songs at that point but remember thinking: 'What! The punk groups play over there?' It just looked like an entrance to some dodgy old bar or something... I dunno, I was only 13 at the time, I had a lot to learn I suppose and I was only really on the first couple of laps into my punk rock circuit. What the hell did I know? Anyway, I just knew that I would have to be visiting that nondescript, almost hidden-away doorway to punk and its sibling cousins hideaway at some point. I had yet to break into the punk live experience but the Limit club was certainly written into my plans.

"The Limit club was mentioned more and more around our circle of school-situated punks. We had now been to the Top Rank quite a few times and seen the many tempting gigs being put on at the West Street joint in the music weeklies. Some of the older lads were going to see groups there such as Penetration, the Adverts, The Police, Lurkers, Undertones etc, but we were constantly being told by the 18-year-olds that there was no chance of us lot getting into the place.

"Their door policies were far stricter than the all-welcome approach of Top Rank's security and box office. As a result, along with other hints of a mysterious aura that was enclosed behind The Limit's closed door, I personally was a little scared of the place but being a teenage punk kid there was no way that I was gonna let on about that!"

Wilco Johnson at The Limit
Photo: Chris Walker

"What! The punk groups play over there? It just looked like an entrance to some dodgy old bar or something."

"Time blurs many old memories and the punk era, in some ways, came and went pretty quickly so I am not entirely sure when my first Limit experience was. I am almost sure that it was on a winter's evening - it was pissing it down, I do know that. I think it was the Vibrators who were playing. I remember going up there with a mate of mine called Ian and when we got there we stood at the other side of the road for a while anticipating our next move. I was wearing black postman trousers with the red piping down the side of each leg, a T-shirt, black donkey jacket and Doc Marten boots. My mate was wearing a German Luftwaffe jacket and I think maybe trainers and a pair of zipped trousers?

"As soon as me and my mate went over, wet through and inwardly feeling a teenage tremble kind of buzz, I saw the doorman/ bouncer look me up and down - totally ignoring my mate's Fifth columnist jacket and staring at my footwear. 'No Dockers!' he says. My heart sank. ' I don't believe this' I thought: 'I have been psyching myself up all day at school for this and just cos of my boots I can't get in.' I could hear one of the groups sound-checking and as the bouncer was telling me my bad fuckin' news I managed to peer past him and could see into the dark abyss of the legendary notorious Limit club. I could see it, feel it, almost taste it but for this time it was not to be. No way were we gonna get in. It didn't appear to be our ages, though, it was our dockers. Christ, how were we gonna kick someone's head in? We were mere kids.

"But we wanted a taste of The Limit club night life. 'You have one of our bands on, c'mon let us in,' were our unspoken words of discontent and disappointment.

" It would have to be a little longer before we would get in there. Maybe even a matinee show - you never know. 'Oh fuck it. Let's piss off back to Rawmarsh and go and catch the last half hour of the youth club instead. The Limit club will have to wait a while."

Richard Chatterton: "I had been wanting to go to The Limit Club for ages but didn't have anyone to go with. I knew that the first band to play there had been Siouxsie and the Banshees. Since my first live punk experience I had attended 35 concerts (I kept a list!) at seven different venues, mostly at the Top Rank and Rotherham Art Centre, in my home town, but also at Sheffield City Hall, the polytechnic and the university.
But I was apprehensive about going to The Limit as it was a club and opened til two so differed from the other venues.

Live action at The Limit

Department S

Nine Below Zero

Polecats

The Cramps

"Most of my friends by then in Sheffield were punks and wouldn't entertain any art school bands or post-punk pretensions, unless Johnny Rotten was in the band, so it was with two friends from Chesterfield, Dawn and Mandy, that I first walked down the hallowed steps to The Limit basement. In later years I thought they should have had a crest atop these steps, like at Anfield, which all the home players touch for luck as they run out on to the pitch. A couple of hard but friendly bouncers ushered us inside. This wasn't small town Rotherham or Chesterfield now, the venue would be bigger, darker and fuller, with people from all over the Steel City inside. I was very excited and nervous.

"I need not have worried. The Limit was dark, yes, but to greet the Bunnymen at their South Yorkshire debut were scarcely a hundred people. The club was so empty that Dawn had the chance to chat awhile with Macca, the Bunnymens' mop-topped iconic lead singer dressed in battered raincoat. She fancied him like mad. The Bunnymen were great and we talked about the gig and venue all the way home. From then on I became a Limit regular, going on Mondays, Thursdays, Fridays and Saturdays.

"Music was incredibly exciting around that time. Punk had liberated rock and roll from 20-minute guitar solos and its manifesto declared anyone could play. The better bands had evolved and realised that you didn't have to stick to punk's original three-minute format but could harness punk's energy to experimentation - reggae, dub, jazz, existentialism, etc. And in Sheffield particularly this involved using synthesisers. Bands were now popping up all over the place. In fact I had become friends with a band called Vena Cava a few months earlier and had been to see them at the Saddle, which was the pub nearest The Limit, on a night when I almost made my first appearance in the club but changed my mind. A pint in the Saddle beforehand became an essential part of The Limit going out ritual. For a while I saw as many local bands as touring ones around this time, may of them at The Limit.

"One night I was immensely proud to be part of the crowd was when Yaboo played. They were formed by a group of people whom I had met in the Fusion in Chesterfield. They were a lively raucous punk funk band with sax and trumpeters in their ranks and should have gone further.

I was always envious of people who had formed bands: even I was in five bands at the same time but never managed to get around to playing a note. My friends band Vena Cava, later St Christopher, who went on to get record-of-the-week from Martin Lilleker in The Star, which was no mean feat as at that time Sheffield's electronic music age was at it's peak, with the Human League, Cabaret Voltaire, ABC, Heaven 17 and the Comsat Angels making the Steel City proud."

Philip Wright: "Bands I saw there included The B-52s, The Skids, The Specials, The Beat, Secret Affair, The Mekons, Gang of Four, Madness, The Barracudas, The Revillos, The Lurkers and many more. I went from wearing a leather bike jacket in my early days to wearing a Mod suit and then just normal stuff, and always used to hang around the stage area with my mates. (At 6ft2ins I was one of the smallest! So if you remember a group of very tall lads it will have been us.) I remember Mick McLean on the door and Andy Dunraven and Louis, plus some lad called Ivan and a really evil looking bloke. The main thing was, of course, the music and even today if I hear a certain record I will think to myself, 'Limit record'. These would include 'I Got you' by Split Enz, 'Tainted Love' by Soft Cell, 'About the Weather' by Magazine, 'Transmission' by Joy Division, 'Furniture Music' by Red Noise, 'Life In Tokyo' by Japan, 'Boys Cry' by Original Mirrors, 'Into the Valley' by the Skids, anything by the Jam. The DJ (Paul 'Legs' Unwin) used to play 'Sunday Papers' by Joe Jackson and say into the microphone: 'If this isn't number one next week I want to know why.' He said it every week but it never got to number one!

"But the one record that above all others, to me, is THE Limit record of all time is 'Quiet Life' by Japan. I only have to hear the opening keyboards and I am once again back in the sweaty, dark, but totally fantastic, Limit Club"

The Warhols
Copyright Steve Stevlor

Copyright Steve Stevlor

LIMIT CL

MAY 7 : DISCO
MAY 8 : T.B.C.
MAY 9 : CHINA STREET
MAY 10 : SQUEEZE
MAY 11 : JAGS + DEAF AIDS
MAY 12 : DISCO
MAY 14 : DISCO
MAY 15 : AFTER THE FIRE
MAY 16 : REGGAE DISCO
MAY 17 : PUNISHMENT OF LUXURY
MAY 18 : SORE THROAT
MAY 19 : DISCO
MAY 20 : DISCO
MAY 22 : ANGLETRAX
MAY 23 : TRIBESMAN
MAY 24 : GARRY BOYLE BAND
MAY 25 : SIMPLE MINDS
MAY 26 : DISCO
MAY 28 : DISCO
MAY 29 : THE CURE
MAY 30 : TRADITION
MAY 31 : THE LURKERS

LIMIT CLUB

MAY 7 : DISCO
MAY 8 : T.B.C.
MAY 9 : CHINA STREET
MAY 10 : SQUEEZE
MAY 11 : JAGS + DEAF AIDS
MAY 12 : DISCO
MAY 14 : DISCO
MAY 15 : AFTER THE FIRE
MAY 16 : REGGAE DISCO
MAY 17 : PUNISHMENT OF LUXURY
MAY 18 : SORE THROAT
MAY 19 : DISCO
MAY 20 : DISCO
MAY 22 : ANGLETRAX
MAY 23 : TRIBESMAN
MAY 24 : GARRY BOYLE BAND
MAY 25 : SIMPLE MINDS
MAY 26 : DISCO
MAY 28 : DISCO
MAY 29 : THE CURE
MAY 30 : TRADITION
MAY 31 : THE LURKERS

Limit ads from NMX fanzine

WHATS ON AT THE

LIMIT

CLUB WEST S

SHEFFIELD

AUGUST 2nd : LEW LEWIS'REFORMER
AUGUST 3rd : THE SPECIALS
AUGUST 4th : DISCO
AUGUST 6th : DISCO
AUGUST 7th : THE ZONES
AUGUST 8th : DISCO
AUGUST 9th : THE TUNES + THE DO
AUGUST 10th : DISCO
AUGUST 11th : DISCO
AUGUST 13th : DISCO
AUGUST 14th : THE DEAF AIDS +
AUGUST 15th : DISCO
AUGUST 16th : DEF LEPPARD
AUGUST 17th : DISCO
AUGUST 18th : DISCO
AUGUST 20th : DISCO
AUGUST 21st : MOD NIGHT - TH
AUGUST 22nd : DISCO
AUGUST 23rd : STARJETS
AUGUST 24th : DISCO
AUGUST 25th : DISCO
AUGUST 27th : DISCO
AUGUST 28th : MOD NIGHT -
AUGUST 29th : DISCO
AUGUST 30th : SHAKE

AN AD FOR

THE LIMIT

70-82 WEST ST.

MARCH 10 : DISCO
MARCH 12 : FREE DISCO
MARCH 13 : JOE JACKSON
MARCH 14 : REGGAE REGULAR
MARCH 15 : SKIDS (2 SHOWS)
MARCH 16 : AFTER THE FIRE
MARCH 17 : DISCO
MARCH 19 : FREE DISCO
MARCH 20 : FREE BAND FESTIVAL
MARCH 21 : PRESSURE SHOCKS
MARCH 22 : SMIRKS (ANNIVERSARY NIGHT)
MARCH 23 : PANTIES
MARCH 24 : DISCO
MARCH 26 : FREE DISCO
MARCH 27 : FRANC BLANC
MARCH 28 : REGGAE/FUNK/SOUL DISCO
MARCH 29 : THE PRETENDERS
MARCH 30 : GANG OF FOUR
MARCH 31 : DISCO
APRIL 2 : FREE DISCO
APRIL 3 : LITTLE BO BITCH
APRIL 4 : WOLFRACE
APRIL 5 : VIOLINSKI
APRIL 6 : T.B.C.
APRIL 7 : DISCO
APRIL 9 : FREE DISCO
APRIL 10 : FAME

CHAPTER SIX

Random brushes

WITH THE **FAME GAME** AND OTHER ODDITIES

The Limit on the silver screen

As the notoriety of The Limit grew, so did its ability to attract the weird and wonderful through its doors.

Nightclubs have always found it notoriously hard to keep 'dead time' to a minimum: it wasn't unusual in the trade to find venues surviving on nothing more than being busy eight hours out of a possible 168 in any given week – only opening from 10pm until 2am every Friday and Saturday night. So it wasn't odd for venues to entertain all manner of things to keep the cash coming in.

The Limit, which was viewed as pretty leftfield to start with, managed to attract everything from a religious cult which used to haul settees and lamp-stands down the stairs every Sunday morning to its own version of The Full Monty for hen parties.

In short, everything from the famous to the infamous crossed the threshold in the club's 13-year reign.

Stars regularly stumbled out of the stage-door of nearby Sheffield City Hall and ended up in the venue, sited just a few seconds' walk away.

One of The Limit's earliest brushes with fame outside of the venue's enviable roll- call of artists was via celebrated writer Barry Hines, the man behind the gritty smash-hit film, Kes.

His flick, 'Looks and Smiles', was shot in the depths of Thatcher's Britain and came out the year before Alan Bleasdale's 'Boys From The Blackstuff' hit television screens.

The film, directed by Ken Loach, was shot in part at The Limit. It tells the story of two unemployed teenagers struggling to find work – a story sadly being played out across Britain at the time.

Phil Staniland: "I remember the auditions for the film that took place at Castle College. I, along with the rest of the student population, went for it. I remember we were auditioning for the nightclub scene that was set to take place in The Limit. Needless to say I didn't get picked!"

Clean-cut American star David Cassidy – hardly a man you'd associate with the subterranean sleaze-feel of somewhere like The Limit – turned up unannounced one night to the amazement of Kevan Johnson.

"David Cassidy came in one night – he'd just played Sheffield City Hall. We'd got a Battle of the Bands on that night. Nice kid. Had a drink with him. Chatted with him. He was a gnat's cock away from getting on stage and having a sing."

The day jobless kids became stars

By Charmaine Spencer

LIFE on the dole brightened up for a day for more than 20 jobless Sheffield youngsters who took part in the new film by Barry Hines, Looks and Smiles.

The film, part of which is being filmed at the Limit Club in the city, tells the story of two unemployed teenagers struggling to find work.

Producer, Irving Teitelbaum, said: "The film is realiy about the lives and experiences and pressures of not being able to find a job. The Bow Centre for jobless kids in Sheffield were extremely helpful to us in providing us with some authentic youngsters.

"It's a local film so we've used local kids. We wanted extras for one scene and we wanted the real people. When people see the film it will be an authentic one."

Being a faceless extra in the film seemed like a God-send to teenagers from the centre in Holly Street. For many of them it was a chance to forget the boredom of being jobless, if only for a day.

Boredom

Richard Swearing, aged 16, of Penrhyn Road, Hunter's Bar, said: "There's nothing else to do is there? It's sort of broken up the boredom for me a bit.

"It's better than being out in the streets, getting into trouble, and I've met loads of different kids here, which isn't bad."

Pete Naylor, aged 17, of Park Grange View, Norfolk Park, said: "If I wasn't taking part I'd probably be mucking around at the Bow Centre or just walking around town."

Joan Sampson, also 17, of Hunter House Road, Hunter's Bar said: "I've made friends here, and it's broken up the boredom of my day for me. If I wasn't here I'd be doing what the others do — just go down to the centre all day just playing music, and that's it."

The film, directed by Ken Loach, will be shown on ATV sometime next year. Said Mr Teitelbaum: "We didn't actually go out looking for unemployed kids, but the Bow Centre was a good source."

Bay City Roller fans go crazy at Sheffield City Hall

Photo: Sheffield Newspapers

Rollermania fails to infiltrate The Limit

Bay City Rollers were one of the biggest things on the planet in the early to mid-seventies.

Though their success was on the wane by end of the decade they could still be relied upon to bring tens of thousands of women across the country to hysteria with one wave of a tartan scarf.

They were more than used to the world and his wife being at their beck and call and bars the world over doing all in their power for a Bay City Roller endorsement. It didn't happen at The Limit.

Glass collector Martin Bellamy was on duty that fateful midweek night.

He said: "I think it was a Wednesday night that the Bay City Rollers must have been playing Sheffield City Hall. The club was virtually empty except for Paul Unwin in the DJ box so we decided to shut the place, it was about 1.30am. Suddenly the Bay City Rollers waltzed in still in their outfits. Nobody was impressed in the slightest.

"The bar staff told them they'd stopped serving and to go home. They obviously realised they weren't going to get any favours at The Limit, they turned and left without saying a word!"

Battle of the bands

Despite The Limit's sometime fractious relationship with local bands (quite understandable in some cases) it was the annual epicentre of action in 1985 as it teamed up with The Gazette and Gold Label to host Sheffield's own band of the year competition.

The November final of 'Band of '85' saw four acts going head to head. Manager Steve Bolderson was impressed by the interest in the event, he told the press at the time.

"We have had a good following ever since the contest started."

Hi'n'Dri, Ministers of Inspiration, The Shirts and Slingshots battled it out for glory.

John Quinn of The Star said things didn't always go as smoothly as they might:

"We'd have judges not turning up, the bar-staff doing the judging and letting their mates win, the losing bands' mothers complaining..."

With £1,000 waiting for the winner, it wasn't surprising there were arguments somewhere down the line.

The event also ran the following year, won by Eliakim with runners-up Two Gun and Night Run.

A 1987 newspaper reports on The Limit's commitment to nurturing local talent "in a bid to revive the city's flagging music scene".

Sheffield guitar-legend Frank White was lined up to open and close a weekly Sunday night session.

A series of Saturday lunchtime concerts featuring up-and-coming talent was also launched, with Agetan Sax lined up for the first one.

Elements of George Webster's regular charity drives at The Buccaneer and then at Wapentake Bar were also still evident.

The Limit ran its own version of Live Aid in 1985 to send money to help the African famine drive, for example.

Six South Yorkshire bands lined up: Who Cares Wins, The Pleasure Men, T-Dive, The Nearly Band, The Risk, Some Party and The Doll House.

and movies page

from Music City

WHO'LL BE OUR BAND OF '85?

SHEFFIELD is Music City.

Hometown to such bands as ABC, the Human League and Saxon, it continues to spawn new talent at an amazing rate - and the Gazette wants to make sure the best of the new bands do not go unrecognised.

We are joining Gold Label lager and The Limit Club in West Street to promote Band of '85, a competition to find the best up-and-coming rock outfit in the area and to reward it with a first prize of £1,000.

Heats are held every Tuesday night at The Limit and next week we shall be bringing readers up to date on the results so far.

There are still some competition places left and any band who fancies their chances can apply to enter by phoning 730940. Three bands compete in every heat and the winners go forward to the next round.

Besides that big £1,000 first prize, there's a second prize of £300, a third of £200, plus a consolation prize of professional studio time to put together a demonstration tape.

Music fans who want to go along to make their own judgments about the bands can get in on contest night for £1 - doors open 9 p.m.

The Human League (top) and Saxon — two of the n... Sheffield bands who made it. Who's next for the big ti...

No poofs in The Limit

The venue's foray into hen-party nights in December 1984 was interesting if nothing else.

The Limit was hired out by stag-party-style comedian Bobby Andrews for "Christmas festivities".

The Dronfield-based entrepreneur was keeping himself busy at the time, having been on duty at a Variety Club gentlemen's evening at Sheffield's Top Rank a few days earlier and having just made a TV commercial for an upholstery firm.

Stephen McClarence's newspaper report of the time for Sheffield Newspapers reads like a Full Monty postscript.

"In the interval, back in their dressing room - a large broom cupboard at the side of the stage - Rocky, Casanova and Mr Olympia reveal how they come to be earning a living in which baby oil could be tax-deductible.

'We were unemployed and there was an advert in Wolverhampton job centre two years ago for male exotic dancers,' says Rocky."

The audience was a far cry from the rebellious punks who were queuing for Siouxsie and the Banshees a few years earlier.

Stephen McClarence continues: "At 9pm, Sheffield's West Street nightspot is hardly rampaging. The women - mostly in their twenties, mostly in groups - sit in their best Tuesday night going out gear, clutching their telescopic brollies."

But star of the show had to be the MC. "The lights change and suddenly it's our host, bouncing bubbly Bobby Andrews, veteran of a thousand stag nights, no gag too mucky, now promoting hen nights.

"Hello girls," he purrs into the microphone. "Ooh, we've got some guys for you tonight - and I'm no poof."

Bobby Andrews and his strippers didn't become a permanent fixture at The Limit.

God gets his rocks off at The Limit

One of the building's most bizarre outside hires, according to club manager Gary Wilson, was early 'meetings' by a Christian group based at St Thomas' Church in the Crookes area of Sheffield.

Later revelations of the gathering that became known as the Nine O' Clock Service went on to make national headlines as a police investigation uncovered evidence of alleged “improper sexual conduct” by leader Chris Brain.

Gary Wilson said: "They'd come down with settees and lamps and things and turn the club into a front-room type of thing.

"The event would start with dance and techno music.

"I remember coming down one Sunday morning just before noon and there was this figure with flashing lights all over it. There were images screened of volcanoes erupting and vast sheets of ice falling into the sea and everybody was going absolutely crazy.

"When the clock struck 12 there was a massive 'bang' and everyone hugged each other."

Hugging was just the start of things, it would appear. Minister Brain ended up quitting after admitting to "improper sexual conduct with a number of women".

One of the female service leaders said of Mr Brain in The Independent in November 1995: "He would regularly talk about how we were discovering a post-modern definition of sexuality in the church."

“Again, its language covering up the fact of what was really going on - one bloke getting his rocks off with about 40 women."

Satan gets his rocks off at The Limit

The venue never really got into metal in any big way.

Probably its most notable foray – besides Def Leppard being regular punters even when they were fast becoming megastars - was a brief stint with Mick and Dez Bailey. Better known as the Bailey Brothers and regularly cited as the inventors of the ‘air guitar’ (their heavy rock DJ shows which started in the late 1970s saw them using imitation wooden guitars as on-stage props) – these two ex-miners from Sheffield's Killamarsh also landed one of the first ever shows on the fledgling MTV music channel.

Limit management enlisted their services to develop a new Friday rock night. Everything from mass devil signage to Miss Wet T-shirt competitions followed in their wake.

The Bailey Brothers said: “We were asked to turn Friday nights at The Limit Club into a rock night. All the rock fans used to go to Rebels on Dixon Lane at the time so dragging their arses up to West Street wasn't going to be easy, especially as they made it free entry into Rebels!

At the time we were doing monthly residencies in Hull, London, Birmingham, Wolverhampton and Derby. We arranged coach trips to the venue from Derby and Wolverhampton and so in no time the Limit was rammed.

Mick Bailey (right) with a Miss Wet T-Shirt hopeful Bailey Brothers collection

"The Beach Boys song Surfing USA was an unusual hit with the fans as we started an indoor surfing craze that started at The Limit. You had to ride on your mates shoulders from one end of the dance floor to the other as if it was a big wave, the audience would end up pulling the surfers off on cue as we shouted 'Watch out for the sharks.' The last one standing at the end of the song usually ended up with a new album from the Baileys.

"It spread to most of our gigs around the UK and was a lot of fun.

"Bon Jovi were kings at the time with 'You Give Love A Bad Name' from their New Jersey album and 'Living on A Prayer' from Slippery When Wet.

"Whitesnake 87 was hot, especially the song 'Still Of The Night' but obviously Def Leppard was a band we have supported since their first EP. Rick Savage (bass guitarist) had given us an exclusive listen to a few songs for the forthcoming Hysteria album in his white Porsche after a game of pool together at the South Sea pub in Broomhill, Sheffield.

"Rick Savage had given us an exclusive listen to a few songs for the forthcoming Hysteria album in his white Porsche after a game of pool together at the South Sea pub in Broomhill."

"Once the Hysteria album was complete he gave us the exclusive track list and title for the magazine we wrote for at the time called Metal Hammer which was appreciated. 'Animal' was well received, as was 'Pour Some Sugar.'

Limit glass collector Martin Bellamy remembers the night well:

"A coach came down from Wolverhampton and this girl got her purse nicked. Everyone had a whip-round and she left with more money then she arrived with."

Bailey Brothers collection

Followers of the Bailey Brothers get down to business at The Limit

"We were asked to turn Friday nights at The Limit Club into a rock night. All the rock fans used to go to Rebels on Dixon Lane at the time so dragging their arses up to West Street wasn't going to be easy."

Bailey Brothers

Mick and Dez Bailey, complete with trademark imitation guitar, in action at The Limit'

Bailey Brothers collection

Pink Floyd nearly perform

One of the biggest bands on the planet had ordered their drinks and was nicely settled in before they were even recognised – despite being some of only a small handful of punters being in the club on a quiet, midweek night.

Martin Bellamy said: "Kevan Johnson didn't recognise them and neither did George Webster – they walked right past them to get in. I didn't clock them at first which was strange because I was actually with them a few years earlier on their 'Ummagumma' album tour. I went with BBC Radio Sheffield to interview them – I was operating the tape machine. Their visit to The Limit was a few years after that and they had abandoned most of their hair by that stage as well.

"They were looking to try new stuff out in front of smaller audiences and see how things worked out."

Pink Floyd never did play The Limit but they definitely mulled it over.

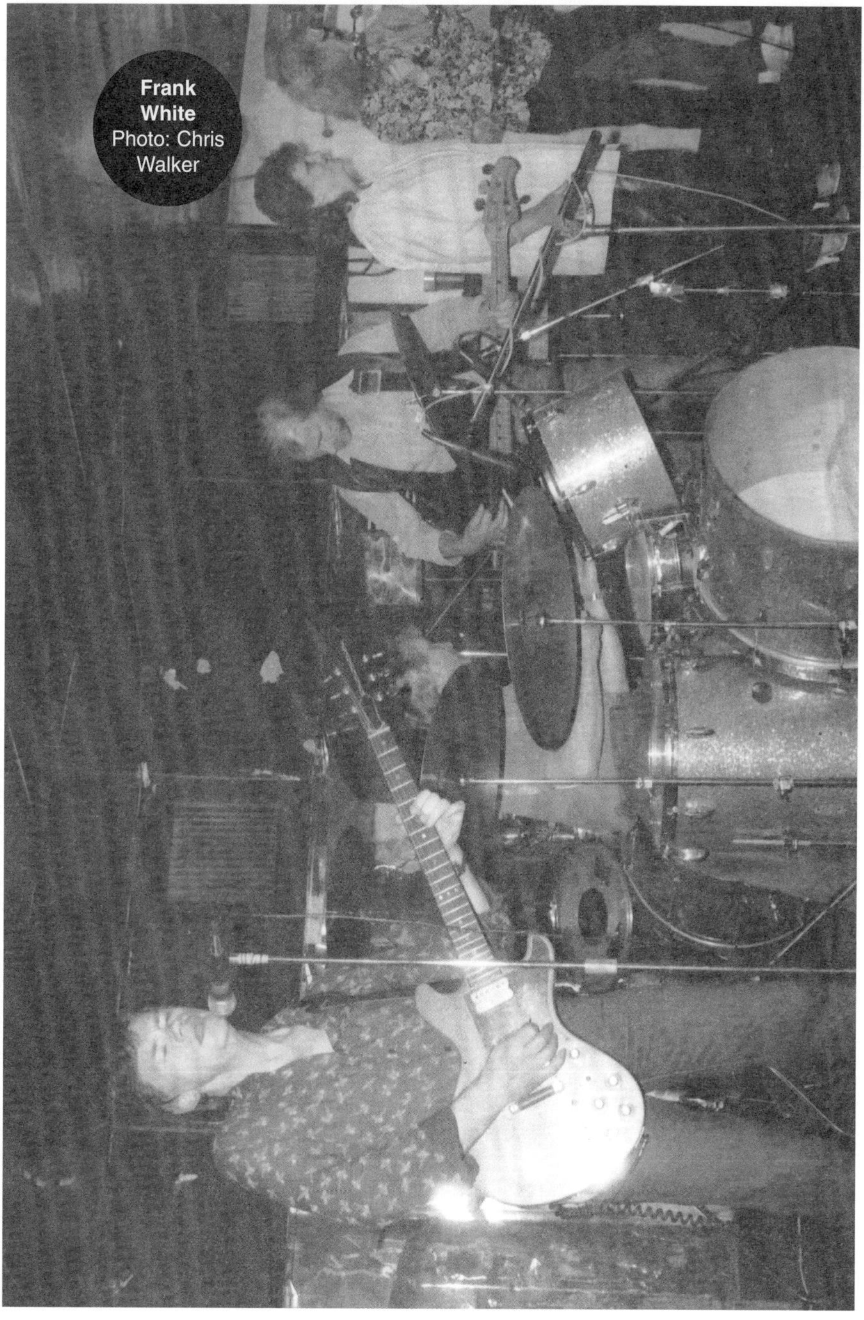

Frank White
Photo: Chris Walker

Limit-goers set sail for Glastonbury in the mid-eighties (left to right - back row) Glen Basford, Si Hagen. (front row) Al Lamb, Dean Rowan, Jake and John Lewis

Limit-goer Jono (left) at Glastonbury

CHAPTER SEVEN

Who wants to be a millionaire?

ENTER THE LYCEUM

As a measure of how much money The Limit was making – and how invincible the management was now feeling - you only have to look at their bankrolling of Sheffield Lyceum.

While the rest of the UK was in full-blown recession, the venue management was eager for new ways to extend their busines empire. Limit manager Steve Bolderson said they were virtually untouched by the economic hardships of the early eighties and the year-long miners' strike which followed.

"We always had a new influx of students every year so we were fine," he said.

But even the steady supply of new customers wasn't enough to meet the financial appetite of Sheffield Lyceum...

Originally opened in 1897 as a theatre, the Lyceum was designed by celebrated architect WGR Sprague and is famous as being his only surviving design outside of London.

The listed Victorian building had fallen into complete disrepair following its closure in the late sixties – it was a bingo club by that stage. There were even calls for the building to be demolished in 1975.

But The Limit owners had other ideas, in a move Kevan Johnson now admits was nothing short of "a bleeding disaster".

It obviously didn't start off that way; in fact it was meant to set up the entire Limit inner circle for life. DJ and Limit manager Paul Unwin remembers it well.

"Kevan Johnson walked into the office one day and said: 'I've just made you all millionaires.'

Right: The Lyceum Theatre, derelict in the mid seventies

Illustration: Ann Beedham

I said how? And he said: 'I've just bought the Lyceum.'"

A stunned silence ensued, by all accounts, until Paul Unwin replied: "It just looks like a big hole to throw money into."

Hole or not, for anyone lucky enough to go to the place when it was run by George Webster and Kevan Johnson and the rest of The Limit team, it truly was a fabulous venue to see live music in Sheffield.

But fabulous comes at a price…

Paul Unwin said: "I remember standing on the stage and looking up… Sheffield Lyceum has fourteen roofs and every one had a hole it."

Kevan Johnson's description was less complimentary even than that.

He said: "There was no roof on it and there was pigeon crap everywhere."

The project was probably the beginning of the end of the partnership for Kevan Johnson and George Webster and certainly created a seismic black hole in their fast-developing wealth.

In fairness you would have expected more support from Sheffield City Council in a move to breathe new life into one of Steel City's most historic landmarks.

Limit management said they got nothing but grief. On the face of it, the Lyceum purchase fitted perfectly into The Limit plan of action that was already in full swing making huge amounts of money from promoting gigs in other, larger venues.

If they owned a big venue themselves, then there'd be no more hire fees.

One of their most famous promotions away from The Limit – and definitely one of the most lucrative – was The Police.

Kevan Johnson said: "We used to book the bands two to three months in advance of their performance. We got a call from the agency one day to say: 'There's a band going on tour called The Police - do you want them?' Nobody had heard of them at that stage but we said 'yeah, how much are they'. They said '£150'. We said 'ok' and the deal was done.

"At the same time Western Jean Company [a shop that used to sit at the top of Fargate] was opening a shop in Houston because they decided they wanted to try their luck in the States, so they invited us all over.

"I'd not been to America before and a big gang of us went. While we were there, unbeknown to us The Police released Roxanne in the States, prior to it being out in the UK, and it went straight to number one.

"We were at this bar listening to this great song and I asked who it was and someone said it was The Police.

"It then dawned on me that the same band was booked to play The Limit in three weeks.

"When we got back it was crash, bang, wallop. The booking agency was on the phone saying: 'The Police can't play The Limit, the song's number one in the UK now.' I asked why not and they said: 'It's not big enough.' Well they couldn't get out of the contract so we ended up going down to Top Rank and booked them in there. I think the whole shooting match ended up costing us £1,000 – we were to take the door and Top Rank the bar. Then we advertised it and we were absolutely mobbed out. In the end we didn't sell any advance tickets and decided we'd risk it with a walk-up.

"When we got back it was crash, bang, wallop. The booking agency was on the phone saying: 'The Police can't play The Limit, the song's number one in the UK now."

The average price for a known band at The Limit was £2 to £2.50. We did The Police at £5 and 3,600 came down, the biggest crowd I think they ever had in the Top Rank. We took somewhere in the region of £16,000 that night in cash and paid the band £150."

The growing reputation of The Limit within the music industry helped them land other big seminal gigs which Sheffield might never have had otherwise.

One of their most famous was The Ramones at the Top Rank

Richard Malik, who travelled from Chesterfield for it, said it was one of the best nights of his life. He said: "I'd been wanting to see The Ramones ever since I heard their first album.

"Me and a bunch of schoolmates travelled over on the train and we were there hours early. I remember various fights kicking off around Pond Street between punks and trendies.

"The gig was totally mental and the performance of the band was relentless – I've never seen a group perform at such break-neck pace. I don't think the band uttered one word between songs – just Dee Dee bellowing out '1234' to kick off each new song. I remember a mass pogo to Blitzkrieg Bop and everyone shouting Hey Ho Lets Go."

Limit DJ and club manager Paul Unwin says George Webster and Kevan Johnson made a small fortune from their outside promotions but, when it should have been setting them up for life, it was actually having a detrimental effect on things.

He said: "Money corrupts doesn't it? And in fairness they made vast amounts of money through outside promotions. I mean The Limit was a licence to print money. It was good for me, don't get me wrong. In Sheffield the average wage at that time was probably £40 a week. In 1978 I was earning over £200 a week. If they had a good night, there was always a bonus on offer somewhere down the line."

According to Unwin, The Limit club ran very well in its early days, probably too well as it gave a feeling that the management had got the Midas Touch.

He said: "The club never ran into any financial difficulties at all but the downside of that was that the management thought they were untouchable as far as business was concerned."

Re-opening a venue like Sheffield Lyceum, which had such an important place in the hearts and minds of local people, should have brought about an air of respectability for The Limit and major plaudits for their efforts.

Unfortunately the opening night was marred by a serious incident involving George Webster himself.

Sheffield Newspapers' story headed 'Lyceum Boss Hurt' of October 7, 1981, said: "George Webster, joint-owner of Sheffield's Lyceum, has a badly broken leg after a city nightclub incident. Partner Kevan Johnson vowed to get Mr Webster to tonight's concert at the theatre by pop group Odyssey, its first show since it was closed 12 years ago."

Sheffield music journalist and author Martin Lilleker suggests the incident set the scene for the short and turbulent life of The Limit-owned Sheffield Lyceum.

He said: "Webster, who lived in a huge house in Stocksbridge, was attacked and an iron bar smashed across his kneecaps behind the back of Uriah Heep's wine-bar on Eyre Street. He ended up in a wheelchair for a while."

Whatever physical injuries the joint-owner had suffered, the total figure it cost both owners to fund Sheffield Lyceum ended up hitting them for nearly £350,000, according to Paul Unwin.

"I think what really annoyed me was that the council didn't want the place open – they wanted to shut it down. Everything we did with that building they complained about.

"We never got any credit for what we did. We restored the building correctly.

"I remember one day when I was the only person in the building, this bloke from the council turned up and said: 'We've got a problem with the colour you've painted the building.'

"So I said: 'What's the problem, it's being painted as it was on the plans.' So he said: 'It's the wrong colour.' 'Well,' I said, 'we've got a big problem then.' And he said: 'Why's that.' 'Because it's the sandstone yellow which is the same colour as your 'eggbox' [the name given to the eyesore that was the Sheffield Town Hall extension bulldozed to make way for the Heart Of The City project] that you've just come from'."

Sheffield Lyceum remained sandstone yellow.

The list of acts Sheffield Lyceum promoted under George Webster and Kevan Johnson's watch (and George Webster when he tried again minus Kevan Johnson with a different bunch of people including Marcus Vere, a future keyboard player with Living In A Box) reads like a Who's Who of the early eighties pop charts and more and includes:

Alexei Sayle
Anti-Nowhere League
Bauhaus
Belle Stars
Blancmange
Boomtown Rats
Bow Wow Wow
Cabaret Voltaire
Clannad
Danse Society
Dave Berry
Eurythmics
Fashion
Frank White
Gary Moore
Human League
Joan Jett
Joe Cocker
Kid Creole
Killing Joke
Kinks
Level 42
Odyssey
Orange Juice
Sandi & The Sunsets
Screaming Lord Sutch
Shakatak
Shalamar
Simple Minds
Southern Death Cult
Spike Milligan
Squeeze
Steeleye Span
Stray Cats
Stiff Little Fingers
Talk Talk
Tenpole Tudor
The Beat
The Clash
The Damned
The Stranglers
Theatre Of Hate
Thompson Twins
U2
Yazoo.

Vernon Price admires the Margaret Thatcher doll used by Spike Milligan in his Sheffield Lyceum performance

One of the key highlights of the Lyceum days for Webster and Limit DJ Vernon Price (who was stage manager at Sheffield Lyceum) was the two-night run for Joe Cocker, performing 19 years after George Webster originally booked him.

Landing the job as stage manager at Sheffield Lyceum was a dream come true for Price, who got to work with some of the biggest names in the music industry.

Vernon, who sadly died from lung cancer in 2007, had the right laid-back persona to deal with the over-inflated egos of some of the stars who performed.

One night he overhead Bob Geldof planning to do a reduced set as he wanted to get away early. Vernon was having none of it.

Joe Cocker on stage at Sheffield Lyceum
Photo: Sheffield Newspapers

"He ordered Geldof to do the full set as this was Yorkshire and people expected value for money," recounts his ex-wife Debbie Albrow.

LYCEUM

Tudor Way, Sheffield 1

Advance tickets from Lyceum Box Office. Open 10a.m.—5p.m. Mon—Sat.
Enclose S.A.E. with postal applications. Cheques payable to — THERMABBE LTD.

Telephone: 754944

Whats on in

SEPTEMBER & OCTOBER

SEPTEMBER		
4th	Yazoo	£3.50 in adv
11th	Simple Minds	£3.50 & £4.00
15th	Level 42	£3.50 & £4.00
18th	Blues Band	£3.00 in adv
20th	Joe Cocker	All tickets £6.50
21st	Joe Cocker	All tickets £6.50
29th	Wishbone Ash	£3.50 in adv

Further Details for this period to be announced

OCTOBER		
6th	The Beat	£3.50 & £4.00
8th	The Kid Creole and the Coconuts Show	£5.00 in adv
12th	Modern Romance	All tickets £3.50
17th	The Damned with Captain Sensible	£3.00 adv & £3.50 door
22nd	Killing Joke	All tickets £3.00
23rd	Squeeze	£3.50 & £4.00
25th	Shakatak	All tickets £4.00
27th	Stiff Little Fingers	All tickets £3.50
28th	Thompson Twins	£2.50 adv. £3.00 door
29th	Bauhaus	All tickets £3.50
31st	Joan Jett & the Blackhearts	All tickets £3.50

Tickets also available from:
Exit Clothing Company

Vernon Price was at Sheffield Lyceum until the bitter end.

Debbie, who worked behind the bar at the venue at the time, said: "George Webster asked Vernon to go and retrieve a telly out of the office when the Lyceum was all locked up. The police were on the scene seconds later as there were security guards looking out on a neighbouring rooftop. The Lyceum was already in the hands of the receivers."

A newspaper report at the time stated Sheffield Lyceum was to remain closed until the company controlling the operation was either sold or restructured.

Even advance talks with Richard Branson couldn't save it – a deal couldn't be agreed with the Virgin boss who was very interested in adding the venue to his growing empire..

Vernon Price and his wife probably left more of a mark on many of the acts than they ever realised. Debbie said: "We had a dog called Sally, a mad springer spaniel that usually came to work with us. She would always get up and crap on the stage, usually when the road crew were setting up the equipment for the next band that was due on that night.

"Vernon had lots of complaints of dog muck on the roadies shoes."

Sheffield Lyceum wasn't the first and wouldn't be the last of the many business ventures entered into by George Webster and Kevan Johnson as The Limit rumbled along in the background.

Plans for a plush restaurant, wine-bar and more were drawn up for Rockingham Street (not far from The Limit on West Street). The Connections project was set to cost about £150,000 and was aimed at businessmen, offering top surroundings.

Paul Young

"It will be something completely different from anything Sheffield has at present," said Kevan Johnson.

The project was looking to service the large numbers of people set to relocate to Sheffield from London to staff the Manpower Services Commission and Midland Bank headquarters, arriving in Steel City in the early eighties.

In April 1981, however, the project hit a brick wall with magistrates throwing out the application after various objections were lodged.

The Limit's management of eighties idol Paul Young faired rather better.

They got to know him through his early gigs at The Limit and worked with him as he began to achieve success through his Q-Tips incarnation before he went on to hit the big-time with the No Parlez album in 1983 and the string of hits from it.

Paul Young with Q-Tips performing in the early days of The Limit' Photo: Pete Hill

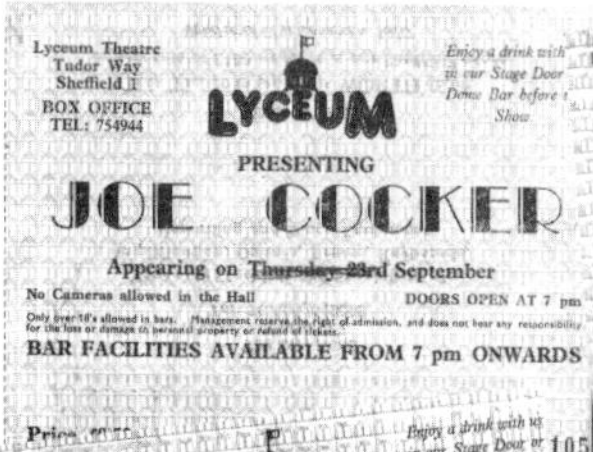

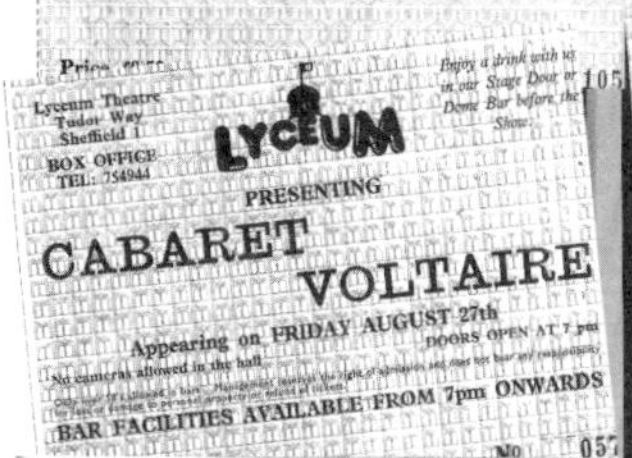

A Flock of Seagulls

Debbie Albrow collection

Photo: Jon Downing

TAKE IT TO THE LIMIT

One of the grand plans – when management were all speaking to each other – was to open up a Limit venue in every major UK city.

If everyone had been pulling in the right direction, it could quite easily have happened.

In fact there's rather a lot that could have been done with the £350,000 estimated to have been ploughed into Sheffield Lyceum* in the early 1980s.

*Sheffield Lyceum reopened as a theatre in 1991 following a £12 million renovation programme. Sheffield City Council had no issue with the colour of the paint or anything this time round.

One of the grand plans - when management were all speaking to each other - was to open up a Limit venue in every major UK city.

The Belle Stars

Debbie Albrow collection

Mick Shedd and Side Effects Photo: Pete Hill

Kevan Johnson in 1982

CHAPTER EIGHT

Eighties club nights, BOUNCERS AND FOOTBALL

The Sheffield after-dark scene changed immeasurably in the 13-year life of The Limit.

New competition soon arose in the shape of The Leadmill, which originally set up as an arts venue; the very short-lived Dingwells, which tried unsuccessfully to poach Limit DJ Paul Unwin; Rebels, opened by former Limit-bouncer Steve Baxendale, and many other venues.

New competition soon arose in the shape of The Leadmill, which originally set up as an arts venue.

But even with the loss of the virtual monopoly it held in the beginning, the massive changes in musical tastes, club nights virtually replacing live acts and whole new generations of punters frequenting the club, what can't really be disputed is that The Limit never lost its legacy and status.

Crap bands, musicians with big egos and the realisation that discos could be far more lucrative than the cost of acts all signalled the death knell for the venue's original identity of six-nights-a-week live music.

Not that these were shelved overnight and in fact they never disappeared totally: it was the weekend live gigs that went first.

DJ Paul Unwin, who shared disc-spinning duties with Manny in the first few years of the club's life, said: "Biggest problem we had as an organisation was that to get the good bands you had to take such a lot of rubbish, so a lot of the time we never made any money by putting on live acts and Kevan clicked on to that fact very quickly.

"The disco was competing with the groups for popularity; George and Kevan soon realised that we could get people in the club on a Saturday night paying two pounds without having to pay for an act."

The bands, on more than a few occasions, didn't really do themselves any favours.

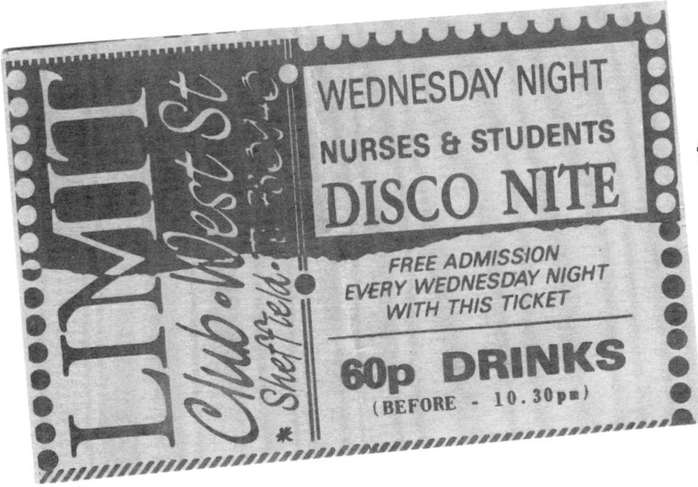

Crap bands, musicians with big egos and the realisation that discos could be far more lucrative than the cost of acts all signalled the death knell for the venue's original identity.

Paul Unwin: "Local bands ended up hating The Limit because they were dealing with business people. Kevan would say: 'If I'm putting on a band I'm giving them a venue, a stage and a big opportunity.'

"Many bands never seemed to click that it was up to them to maximise that opportunity and go out and sell themselves and bring the punters in.

"We'd have bands turn up with say 50 of their entourage and they'd say 'we've had a great night' and we'd think 'well you might have but we certainly haven't', considering we'd be having to pay bar staff, security and

Local rockers

Limit DJs and MTV stars The Bailey Brothers fire up the crowd at Donnington Park's massive Monsters of Rock event
Photo from the Baileys'collection

cover all the other overheads of running a venue like The Limit."

The biggest egos often came with the bands that were on their way up but weren't quite there.

New wave rising stars of the late 1970s the Fabulous Poodles did themselves no favours when they visited.

Paul Unwin: "We'd agreed on a fee of £200

The first wave of Limit club night goers of the early '80s were the punks, mods, goths, indie kids, students, rockers, with a good dose of fist-wielding townies thrown in for good measure at the weekend.

but they decided they wanted a crate of beer as well. Kevan said; 'They're an unknown quantity, I've not signed any rider and they're not getting anything.'

"Being the businessman he was he just saw it as giving away his profit.

"The band were totally obnoxious and they had a massive rant about money. They were also on a percentage of the door-take and put their own guy on the door with a clicker to count how many people came in.

"I told him he couldn't count people with Limit for Life passes [which entitled the chosen few to free entry forever]. The band thought we were fiddling them and the lead singer marched up to Kevan and said: 'You're just another fat-bellied business man.'

"They didn't get their beer and they didn't get another gig at The Limit."

But for many Limit punters who were too young to catch the early years, the club nights of the 1980s were as memorable and popular as any band.

Though the core of Limit-goers were Sheffield, South Yorkshire and North East Derbyshire, club-goers would travel from all over England and even overseas in some cases.

The first wave of Limit club night goers of the early '80s were the punks, mods, goths, indie kids, students, rockers, with a good dose of fist-wielding townies thrown in for good measure at the weekend.

Considering it was such a mix of youth cultures that would ordinarily be tearing lumps out of each other anywhere else, trouble was pretty nominal in the early days of the club thanks to the zero-tolerance attitude of the security, which normally wiped out trouble within seconds of it starting.

Limit goers (left to right) Amanda, Liz and Tracy Pidd

While The Limit was pretty much the master of its own destiny in its formative years, thanks to it leading on the Sheffield synth explosion that dominated the UK in the early '80s and to it being at the forefront of the UK-led punk and ska scene before that, it

Early acid house followers in Sheffield

Photo: Geoffrey Beattie

came as a bit of shock when things abruptly came to halt.

DJ Paul Unwin said: "By 1985 the music scene that had inspired the place was on its arse. Their last influential band had been The Smiths."

Anyone who has ever been a DJ knows how hard it is to fill a dance floor one night a week, let alone doing that five or six as he was.

Add to that the major changes going off both nationally and internationally in the music scene in the early to mid-eighties and it's not surprising he was feeling jaded with the place.

Paul Unwin said: "The Limit became a necessary evil for me. After three years I wanted to leave."

One of the biggest changes of the era was the rise of the 1981-launched MTV and the music video.

The channel, amongst other things, was largely responsible for the global rise of big-hair rock and bands like Sheffield's own Def Leppard, Motley Crue, Poison, Bon Jovi and scores of others that started dominating the UK charts in the 1980s and became one of the most influential music genres of the era. Steel City did play a large part, as it happens; the one-time Limit DJs The Bailey Brothers presented the channel's fledgling rock show.

The Limit also installed one of the first video screens in the region to play the new videos – punters were known to just stand there and gawp at it in the early days.

John Robb, journalist and front man of Goldblade, said: "I used to go to some goth night there They had video screens really early on and I remember Iggy Pop's 'Five Foot One' was always on the screen."

The Live Aid concert of 1985 made a legend out of Bob Geldof and ensured there'd be no chance of him losing any sleep after his early attempt to short-change Sheffield Lyceum punters with a reduced Boomtown Rats set, rumbled by stage manager and occasional Limit DJ Vernon Price.

The Limit staged their own Live Aid style event in 1985.

Hip hop was evolving, gaining recognition and starting to influence.

Punk rock had splintered into sub-genres with people turning veggie and protesting against everything or simply going skateboarding instead.

The influence of house music was coming to fruition as was techno.

The weekly roster at The Limit was a regularly changing, evolving mix of nights with some having longer life spans than others.

The Limit also installed one of the first video screens in the region to play the new videos - punters were known to just stand there and gawp at it in the early days.

'Watered down piss'

We'll probably never know if the beer in The Limit was watered down or not but the debate over its H_2O content was definitely common currency throughout the 1980s and still pervades today on message boards dedicated to the venue.

Most club-goers kept their thoughts between themselves. Others simply avoided the issue by getting loaded in nearby bars like the Saddle, Beehive or Hallamshire and stuffing enough alcohol in hidden pockets and handbags to last them until 2am.

One man was rather more vocal with his thoughts on the beer and it didn't go down well at the time.

Martin Lacey, editor of NMX fanzine, said: "When I started NMX in February '79 I swapped advertising for free admission and permission to sell the mag in The Limit. I was an idealist and an anarchist: I considered music should be by the people, for the people, and anyone trying to get rich off it - promoters, record companies, rock stars - were class enemies and fair game. I also had no qualms about biting the hand that fed... I slagged The Limit off mercilessly, figuring George and Kevan didn't actually read it. I eventually got banned, maybe 1981, for calling their beer 'watered down piss' in print..."

Club-goer Rich Walker found rather simpler ways to be sure of his alcohol content in the club. He took to "sitting and drinking 60p bottles of Newcastle Brown Ale because we knew they couldn't water them down".

He could also get a complimentary nicotine fix following his tour of duty at local bars.

"Monday night Marlboro night, free cigarette on the door lit by a girl in a Marlboro sash and a pack of 5, then a Marlboro-sponsored band. I seem to remember seeing In Tua Nua there but went for the free fags really.

"Always went to the Hallamshire at first but later the Washington, usually Wednesday (nurses and students) but mostly Thursday (goth) never at a weekend though. I lived in Broomhill so walked there and back."

Despite the thoughts on the beer, there were plenty of club-goers to fill Martin Lacey's place at the various bars inside.

Jayne Walton's pre-Limit pub-crawl would put many punters to shame. That's after Ms Walton senior had got her clothes ready to hit the road.

"My mum used to make me a new skirt every week from a yard of material that I got from the market, new shoes from Rebina or the Setts Market. Once in town via the bus we would start in the Queens Head, Barrow Boys, Marples, Mulberry, Brown Bear, Wapentake, Hallamshire, The Saddle, Limit!! We used to catch the 2-o'-clock bus home. I can never forget the police escorts cos the windows always got put through. I will always remember a posh bloke slagging us off and our mate tying his tie to the bus seat rail and setting it on fire!!

"Lots of Boots hairspray, that was the best, perfect wild make-up and never having to worry about somebody wearing the same thing!! Several drinks later - floppy hair, smudged make-up, and a bruise or two from the wild chicken-wing dancing, never had a sad night in there, always different.

"I saw Peter and the Test Tube Babies, Macc Lads, Dr and the Medics, Guana Bats, Terry and Gerry, Killing Joke, Human League, loads and loads...

"It was the only punky place around at the time. Dingy. Dark. Sticky. Flooded. Smelly, the music and the people..."

"I grew up in The Limit, my friends and I worked behind the bar in the middle '80s mainly because that meant we got in for free and the 12 quid we got for three shifts paid our rent. So many memories, from the glass collector who looked like Max Wall, who brought us gifts every week, usually sparkly nail polish; hot Red Stripe; the goth box and its strange dwellers; the boys sat on the stairs having to take their Doc Martens off before they could go in; getting my bag nicked by a skanky skinhead and the bouncer's wife giving me a fiver to get home; poppers - the toilet always smelled of them; being able to get in from being 14...

"It was the only punky place around at the time. Dingy. Dark. Sticky. Flooded. Smelly, the music and the people... the Leadmill

Limit goers - from Paul Unwin collection

tried but it was never the same. Rebels was for the rockers, Club With 2 Brains tried but never quite made it. I remember the cheap drinks, even though they contained 70% extra water; the many bands that didn't play anywhere else; the people - I made many many friends who I still see today... I loved The Limit and so did my hubby.

"And the people - everyone was different. Punks. Rockers. Goths. Gays. Students. And your everyday bloke on the street (usually a mate of the above)."

Weekend action

Barnsley girl Mandy Alleyne was a big Saturday night fan: "I have had some fabulous times at The Limit. Sometimes I'd go three times a week but Saturday was the best night to go, I sometimes think I lived at The Limit, I went that much.

"The club had a great atmosphere, an anything-goes kinda place. I made a lot of friendships there.

"And the people - everyone was different. Punks. Rockers. Goths. Gays. Students. And your every-day bloke on the street."

"The first time I ever went I remember it made such a big impression I was hooked; coming from Barnsley I'd never seen anywhere like The Limit, it was awesome. Don't get me wrong, it wouldn't win any awards for decoration but I didn't mind: the people and music were enough to ignore it all. The music was awesome. They played music you wouldn't hear in other clubs - The Cramps, Sisters of Mercy, Macc Lads - and when King Kurt was played the place went mad, it was a sight to see.

"As for the people, well there were punks - I started out that way then decided to have a flat top, it was awesome,

Phil Staniland (second from right) with Sheffield band Mirror Crack'D when he wasn't having problems with seating arrangements at The Limit

"I changed my appearance several times, it was fun and imaginative - also there were goths, the odd skinhead and gay, straight, anything went really, I met some really great people. The clothes as well: I seem to remember we wore leather mini-skirts, ripped tops and fluorescent socks and plain black pumps. Also cardigans seemed popular; shoes - definitely went to Rebina shoes, anybody remember them? Also bought a lot of clothes from Pentangle in Barnsley and of course my old faithful leather-studded biker jacket and studded dog collars and belts... And leggings have been in for ever more. Typical night: start off down at Dove and Rainbow then off to Golden Ball, Hallamshire, then Frog and Parrot, then back to Hallamshire then finally to The Limit. We would dance the night away and drink loads of Newcastle Brown. We'd also go the Wimpy sometimes and then I used to stay at a friend's before I moved to Sheffield. Now I'm living back in Barnsley, The Limit is no more but it will always live on in my memory. It was the best club ever. It was a sad day when it closed: shame that future generations will miss out on such a great club; there's none to compare."

Sticky floors and vomit

Alison Leeming (formerly Alison Jordan) like many remembers being permanently stuck to the floor.

"My main recollection of The Limit is of sticking to the floor on a Monday night - it was an amazing consistency of blood, beer and vomit!

"And as I worked at the dole office on West Street I walked up past The Limit every Friday morning for years and there was always an obstacle course of splatters to avoid which indicated how busy the club had been on the Thursday night. The number of splatters generally corresponded to the number of assault or injury reports in Friday's Star.

"I love Sheffield and miss it as I now live far far away and I miss my youth on occasion, but I don't miss tiptoeing up West Street on a Friday morning."

Seating problems

Club regular Phil Staniland obviously wasn't regular enough (or maybe sober enough) to realise the chairs weren't quite what they seemed.

He said: "I had been short-changed at the Hallamshire Hotel one night while doing the West Street crawl and had to wait while they emptied the tills at the very end of the night to get my tenner back or however much it was. Even if it was only a tenner in those days that was a lot when you were on the social circuit. We were in quite a big group that night and everyone else had gone down to The Limit so I made my way down a bit later after the finance issue had been cleared up. When I got down there they were all sat in groups around the tables and there were no places left for me. I saw a young couple sat together on a smaller table in front of them that had one spare seat free. 'I'll get that chair,' I thought, 'and go and sit with the others.' I went up to the couple and said: 'Is anybody sat here?' They both looked at me very very oddly, which I couldn't understand at first, and said: 'No there isn't.' So I grabbed hold of the chair and tried to lift it. The couple looked even more perplexed.

"Not having the strength of Godzilla I was unable to move the chair at all. Of course I'd forgotten that all the seats in The Limit were bolted down to the floor.

"Cockney Chris, who was always in The Limit and probably was the only Cockney who ever went in, had been watching this as everyone else had and shouted really loud in his Cockney accent: 'Someone cob 'im a fackkin screw driver!' This was met with hysterical laughter by everyone who was sat in that vicinity. I then realised why the couple had been looking at me very strangely and quite rightly. They thought I wanted to sit with them!"

Auld Lang Syne

Richard Chatterton: "Limit nights were great: piling in with your mates, wandering around looking for people you knew (girls mostly), going up on the wooden stage bit at the side with the chairs, sitting on the stage... I can recall being on the stage on New Year's Eve 1980, after deciding to go out to celebrate on my own, hoping someone I knew would be inside, and singing Auld Lang Syne holding arms with the people alongside.

"I chatted a few times with Jarvis about his band (even once interviewing Pulp in the Hallamshire when it was heaving with a strong Scottish miners contingent in Sheffield for a rally during the miners' strike). I would also watch Trevor Howcher, self-styled 'most beautiful man in the world', saunter by with his entourage, small girls in Boy George dresses.

"The Limit, like other provincial northern clubs such as Erics in Liverpool and the Hacienda in Manchester, had its fair share of characters and have-a-go heroes."

Jack Duckworth's house

Phil Staniland: "The brickwork outside looked like something off the side of Jack Duckworth's house."

"I would also watch Trevor Howcher, self-styled 'most beautiful man in the world', saunter by with his entourage, small girls in Boy George dresses."

DJ Paul Unwin in residence at The Limit Paul Unwin collection

The Limit bouncers

Sheffield's West Street has always been a force to be reckoned with in terms of after-dark action.

It has traditionally been one of the city's main drinking thoroughfares and the last place you'd ever go if you fancied a quiet candlelit dinner on a weekend.

If you were opening a venue along there you normally had to be geared up to expect the worst.

In fact original Limit bouncer Martin Bellamy said the police agreed to turn a blind eye to a few cases of over-zealous justice being handed out by door-staff in the early weeks of the club so that it quickly built a reputation for not tolerating trouble.
It did the trick in no uncertain terms.

The bouncers were a bit too quick to deal with what they saw as trouble in the early days.

The antics of the punk movement all came as a bit of a shock, especially the pogo and slam-dance.

Former NMX editor Martin Lacey said: "The Limit was the first place where the punks and weirdos and musos could go after pub closing in relative safety and with relatively decent music.

"Having said that, I went with a gang of mates on maybe the second or third night The Limit was open. When we started pogo dancing the bouncers went crazy and started throwing as many people out as they could get hold of, one uttering the immortal words; 'If you want to do that go to the Penthouse. This is a nightclub!' I think it took them about 24 hours to realise that if they pursued that policy they would have a very empty club and it was changed accordingly."

In fact original Limit bouncer Martin Bellamy said the police agreed to turn a blind eye to a few cases of over-zealous justice being handed out by door-staff in the early weeks of the club so that it quickly built a reputation for not tolerating trouble.

Martin Bellamy said things could actually be worse than that. "When the security first saw people slam-dancing in the club they immediately thought it was a big fight, waded in, and gave the culprits a good kicking.
They'd no idea what was going on."

Former medical photographer and martial arts aficionado Ivan

Bouncer turned glass collector Martin Bellamy (right) with John and Alison Waldron

Martin as he is today

Bradley became one of the main door-staff by accident.

"I was in the club one night in the early days and some nasty fighting erupted and I knocked a guy out with a fairly clean punch. Kevan was watching and he invited me into the office and offered me the job – it paid more than I was getting as a medical photographer."

He was joined by butcher turned bouncer Chris Baker, who also supplied the meat for The Limit burgers in the early days. "They were the best burgers you could ever get – pure lean meat," says Ivan.

Now it's all well and good having a security team with a formidable (almost mythical in one case) reputation but it regularly served as a green-light invitation to the more unhinged of the community to try their luck DJ Paul Unwin said: "Chris Baker was followed home one night after The Limit. He dished it out a lot but that night he got out of his car and had his face re-arranged with a starting handle."

Bouncer legend Trinny Morris - from Paul Unwin collection

It wasn't always just the security staff who got involved either.

"There were plenty of staff who weren't doormen at The Limit who would join in with the violence," admits Paul Unwin.

In fact non-security staff regularly became targets for violence, both inside and outside the club.

DJ Paul Unwin, who was also the former manager, said there was little choice but to keep fit in order to be prepared in case the worst did happen.

"We all used to train and keep fit because, when it did kick off, it really kicked off and could get very nasty. I trained with a guy called Dave Cook who was a boxer."

There's no doubt there soon became a status attached to being a Limit bouncer but it didn't work in favour of one aspiring hardman.

DJ Paul Unwin said: "We had a glass collector who was always asking me if he could work on the door. I said: 'No, you're a glass collector.'

"He used to ask me every single week and I always said 'no'.

"He came in one night and his head was about twice its normal size. I said: 'What on earth have you done – get to hospital.' I seriously thought he'd been hit by a car or something.

"He said: 'I was coming into work tonight on the bus and this kid asked me if I worked on The Limit door. I said yes.' And the kid beat him senseless."

First and last of the Apaches

Martin Bellamy: "One night some bloke tried to pull half Paul Unwin's DJ box down; he was stood there waving it around at manager Steve Bolderson.

"I walked around the back and shoulder-charged this kid down but when I got up I found I'd torn both the front and back of the top of my blue jeans and I had to spend the rest of the night having these big flaps of denim hanging down each side of my arse. I looked like an Apache Indian."

The legend of Trinny Morris

No incident entered Limit folklore with quite the speed of the stabbing of Trinny Morris. Martin Bellamy arrived at work that night to find blood everywhere.

He said: "I asked: 'What's all this blood?' And I got the answer: 'Oh, Trinny got stabbed.'

"This youth had been thrown out for doing something and two minutes later he came back and said to Trinny 'oh sorry mate' and gestured to tap him on the hip. The next thing Trinny knows this guy has pushed a blade two inches into his stomach.

"So Trinny's rushed to hospital."

The staff were left in a state of shock at The Limit. Things had got violent but nothing had ever happened like that. Certainly not to Trinny: his reputation for being able to handle himself was legendary.

The staff got far more of a shock two days later. Trinny reappeared, stitched up and hell-bent on getting straight down to the business of finding the kid who had stabbed him.

The incident hadn't phased him one iota but realisation of just whom he'd stabbed definitely dawned on the youth in question.

"This kid must have been the only person in Sheffield that didn't know who Trinny was. There was absolutely no doubt he was going to be found but he ended up turning himself in; he obviously realised he was far safer with the police than if Trinny got him," said Martin Bellamy.

Steve Bolderson said the security always did a great job. "If you went into The Limit to cause trouble you weren't going to last long – the team on the door were phenomenal."

Football:

The worst incident of violence involving The Limit was football-related. Steve Bolderson saw it all unfold in front of his eyes.

"There was a bunch of LUFC supporters who got a load of scaffolding poles from over the road and tried to ram the doors. We were behind them when scaffolding poles came flying through them.

"It was as near as we came to a full scale riot: we just had to try and keep the doors locked.

Martin Bellamy admits it was a really nasty incident. "It all started off inside the club. The doormen managed to force them out but they re-grouped outside the club and managed to charge back through the doors and back down the stairs. I grabbed one of them by the neck, another fell at my feet so I stood on his head."

The appearance of LUFC fans was one of the few times the local firms of SWFC (OCS) and SUFC (BBC) fought a common enemy rather than each other.

Deano [from Wookie website]:

"Remember one particular night early '80s, few of us Blades (me, Mick, Smeds, Black Paul, Webby) and about 15-25 others had been in about 30 mins having a drink with a few Wednesday fans who we talked to (black Duggie, Heathy, Darren, Higgo) when all of a sudden loads of lads started coming in Lacoste and Pringled up, after about 15 mins they had filled bottom end. Then the lot went up first time BBC and OCS ever joined together also Trinny, Louie rest of bouncers, never forget sight of Tank launching benches like balsa wood, a lot of the Leeds mob in a bad way, of all the clubs in Sheffield to come and cause trouble in, what nights."

Richard Chatterton admits football was to blame for a rise in violence.

He said: "As the '80s moved on The Limit had gained an aura of trouble when the football fans started bringing their grievances inside. I once was just about to enter and a large group of lads dashed out, then turned around to face the doorway and one of them grabbed my shoulder to involve me and said: 'Come on Wednesday, let's get the bastard pigs.' Not wanting to get involved in something in which I might get hurt and being a keen Blade myself (a pig in their eyes) I quickly shook off the hand and went inside. The '80s was the zenith of football hooliganism and it was seeping into The Limit unfortunately."

More memories:

John Quinn: "The Limit was a legend among a certain section of Sheffield's youth in the late 1970s and for the entirety of the '80s.

"As documented on songs like Mis-Shapes by Limit-regulars Pulp, the city centre in those days could be a hard place - especially at night - if you didn't fit in with the common herd.

"To paraphrase a quote on the sleeve of that single, you could all-too-easily find yourself in the situation where your very existence attracted the attention and abuse of a group of identically-dressed moustachioed meatheads. And the men could be even worse.

"So everyone in any way 'alternative' tended to hang about in the same few venues.

John Quinn today and (inset) in his Limit days

"Rumour has it that when it opened in 1978 it was considered quite swanky. However, by the time I made my Limit debut in 1983 you could drop the 's'."

Goths, punks, gender benders (well it was the '80s) and just general weirdos would flock together, along with quite normal-looking kids who just didn't fancy their chances if fights broke out.

"There just wasn't the plethora of places to go at night that there is nowadays anyway, and there were several into which no-one even slightly off the wall would dare to tread.

"So after you'd been to the Hallamshire, Washington, Hornblower or even Mr Kites, there were more-or-less three choices. If you'd had enough you could get a late bus home or stand around waiting for the mythical taxis that local people seemed to think picked you up after closing time - it appeared that there was an element of alcohol-induced amnesia involved, as the very same people who had wasted a large chunk of the previous weekend standing about on street corners sticking their hands out in vain now seemed to think that one would automatically appear as soon as they had left the pub.

"The third alternative was you could stay in town and try and find somewhere to continue the action. However, there was a serious lack of late-night places to go, certainly in the city centre.

"Nowadays you can spend all night dancing, laughing, drinking and loving - and probably even get a taxi home - but licensing hours were very different then and 2am was the latest time that venues could stay open until. Eeh, we had it tough.

"Out of the few venues open past the witching hour, some required you wore shiny shoes and a tie to even get in, whereas even the ones with a more lenient dress-code seemed to play nothing but the lowest-common-denominator chart hits.

"So that left a .lot of us heading down West Street to The Limit, a pit of a place but also perversely verging on perfect. If we define 'the limit' as being 'as far as something can go', you would be hard-pressed to find any venue in Sheffield with less home comforts, despite the best efforts of the Wapentake and Rebels, both of which had a completely different crowd anyway.

"Rumour has it that when it opened in 1978 it was considered quite swanky. However, by the time I made my Limit debut in 1983 you could drop the 's'.

"From the hazardous path down the stairs when entering the place (there were rumours of the existence of a lift, but no-one I knew had ever seen it) to the sheer stickiness of the floors and the delightful decor (er, black), it wasn't the sort of place you'd want to take your parents, unless you genuinely wanted them fearing for your sanity. And I'm not even mentioning the toilets. Because just thinking about them is bad enough.

"Some of us are unlikely to get over The Limit. It was an utter dive. But it was OUR utter dive. Oh yeah, and I had my first ever proper snog in there. Twenty six years on, I'm still waiting for the second..."
John Quinn

"But there were three bars where you could drink to forget. To forget that at some point you might have to go into the toilets, that is.

"They should really have supplied wellies at the door.

"Nevertheless sometimes it was by far the best night in Sheffield - even knocking its only real rival in those days, the Leadmill, into a cocked hat. Whatever a cocked hat is. Admittedly on some other nights it resembled the Black Hole of Calcutta with beer, and I wouldn't have wished it on my worst enemy, but the thing is that you could just never tell beforehand.

"On an average night you would hear the same songs, often in the same order, and the clientele seemed to be more-or-less unchanging. I'm convinced that some people went there every single night. But there was usually a sense of community about it.

"Of course, there was sometimes trouble (I was once completely minding my own business and someone swung a punch at me. luckily his alcohol intake and the darkness meant that he missed) but the proportion of dickheads was relatively low compared to other places. And the staff usually quickly and efficiently dealt with anyone out for the wrong reasons anyway.

"The music was a fair selection of the sort of stuff you were unlikely to hear in any other place in the city.

"The best punk, electronic and even straight dance stuff would get an airing and even if you didn't like a particular number there was bound to be one you liked coming along in a couple of minutes.

"They had live acts on too, often ones who would become quite big later on. The likes of U2, Madness and UB40 all appeared there early in their career, while on a local level the aforementioned Pulp appeared several times in their early days, including an infamous occasion when Jarvis appeared on stage in a wheelchair after falling from a window.

"However history doesn't record how he actually got into the place in the dark days when disabled access wasn't a consideration anywhere.

"Apparently in their early days The Human League and Def Leppard once played on the same bill but, even after topping the charts on both sides of the Atlantic, the League did a show on the lowdown stage.

"When it closed in 1991 it was like a part of Sheffield's cultural history had been wiped out.

"Some of us are unlikely to get over The Limit. It was an utter dive. But it was OUR utter dive.

"Oh yeah, and I had my first ever proper snog in there. Twenty six years on, I'm still waiting for the second..."

The changing face of The Limit- clubbers in 1989 Photos: Damian Wilkinson

Max the glass collector:

Pip, former Limit barman, said: "Yes it is true Max the glass collector did go around in bicycle shorts. Max was not his real name, he was called Max due to his striking resemblance to Max Wall, mainly due to the hairstyle they shared.

"It's a bit of an irony that they were called glass collectors as the club only served drinks in plastic. We were not even allowed to give out bottles over the bar (except to the bouncers). I guess this was to remove the risk of broken glass.

"Because of the robust nature of the plastic glasses, the collectors could stack them up to extraordinary heights, only limited by the height of the ceiling (sorry couldn't resist the pun!). If the club was crowded, you could always spot Martin [Bellamy] or Max by looking for the telltale signs of the plastic towers moving around round the club, poking up above the punters heads."

More memories:

Keith Strong, former entertainment reporter on The Star, said: "I had a great fondness for The Limit, staff and crowd. I believe the club provided a service close to what the old Black Swan achieved by booking a lot of acts which would find greater fame and wasn't afraid to put on names that hardly anyone had heard of. There were many regulars for the different musical genres who loved their stuff and it was mostly all very good-natured - I don't recall any serious trouble there. People went because they knew to expect a decent standard of artist and not have to worry about being glassed or bottled.

"There was punk, post-punk, New Wave, electronic/synth pop, ska, rock, blues...

"I was particularly impressed with Chris Rea who had blues roots and made his debut with 1978 album Whatever Happened to Benny Santini? He wasn't (still isn't) a dynamic performer but the songs were quality and his guitar-playing exceptional, especially on slide. Might have been on his second Limit appearance but he was very depressed and even talked of quitting. Fool (If You Think It's Over), from the album, had done well in the US but not UK and Elkie Brooks would have the hit in 1981. Thankfully, he finally cracked it in the UK.

"In the same musical vein, Robert Cray was a very welcome visitor from the US. Fine blues singer/guitarist supported on the night by the local Frank White Band in whom I claim a personal interest as my wife was one of his back-up singers. That was an outstanding night despite Frank disappointing everyone (inc Mr Cray) by stubbornly refusing to play to his full potential.

"Jayne/Wayne County & the Electric Chairs were somewhat contrasting US talents.

"The transsexual, who had been part of the early punk wave, had 1978 EP Blatantly Offensive which he/she lived up to in campy/toilet humour way. Quite clever, though, if you weren't of a sensitive nature.

"I'm fairly sure that John 'Moon' Martin came over from the US, too. He's a singer/guitarist/songwriter who composed Bad Case of Loving You (Doctor Doctor) which Robert Palmer had a hit with, and Cadillac Walk, a success for Willy DeVille who just died. Moon was credited as author of three-minute pop novels and proved so. Very enjoyable.

"Q Tips were a blue-eyed soul revelation for me. Lasted only about three years but singer Paul Young went on to much bigger things wherever he laid his hat.

"Local bands acquitted themselves quite well at The Limit with Human League and the Lepps among them. I remember Leppard pestering George for a gig and being given one of the (free) local nites on a bill that included the League.

"I wasn't into the electronic stuff but I thought The Naughtiest Girl Was a Monitor (originally a duo) had something going for them, but they had a surprisingly short career. Think Limit was one of their earliest gigs."

QTips Photo: Pete Hill

Wilko Johnson band at The Limit Photo: Chris Walker

Limit-goer Jono said: "I first remember coming across The Limit when I was a 13/14-year-old in '81 or '82. I was a young punk at the time and remember being well chuffed because I'd managed to get in and looked older.

"I can remember the Human League and Visage being played and lots of lads and lasses caked in make-up dancing with their arms out by their side, I'd call it flouncing for want of a better word. The New Romantics had arrived. I hated it with a vengeance and it was a couple of years before I ventured back.

"I remember venturing in again when I was about 16 and had just started work on a YTS painting-and-decorating scheme - £25.00 a week, a fiver board & lodging (cheers mum) and the rest was expendable income - Limit money. I was hooked.

"I'd be in there every Monday, Thursday, Friday and Saturday. Monday and Thursday were the 50p-a-pint nights up until 11'o'clock and everybody would crowd the bar about 10.45 and buy two or three pints before the price went up. It was the worst lager known to mankind. I can remember Max the glass collector, a 6ft6 version of Max Wall, who used to dress up in a Nazi uniform but wearing shorts – surreal. You would put your pint down on a table and then turn around and see Max legging it with your pint – cheeky fucker.

"I used to meet up with my mates in the Hallamshire on West Street before The Limit - Glen Basford, Deano, Bolty, Al Lamb, Suv, South, Si Hagan, Gaz Pattison, Shaun 'stix' Williams, Miffy, Johnny Taylor, Fleg, Shirley and Hooley RIP. Gaz and Johnny were miners and would come off the afternoon shift and go straight to The Limit.

"They would have dust residue stuck in their eyelashes and would look for all intents and purposes like they were wearing eyeliner. We would take the piss by asking the DJ to play some Soft Cell for Gaz or Johnny.

"Shaun and Miffy were in an anarcho band called Systematic Annexe but any strict punk doctrines used to be put aside when you went in the Limit and they would often be seen talking complete shite to some of the gorgeous goth lasses that used to go in.

"Si Hagan and me were in a band called Toxic Toys (also John and Jake) and we used to have a practice room bang at the side of The Limit.

A dodgy Limit goth

"I can also remember going in The Limit early one Monday night after band practice to take advantage of the 50p-a-pint offer. There was hardly anybody in and I asked a lad for a cig. He gave me the remnants of a roll-up he was smoking. I managed about two drags before it burnt my lips and I put it out on the floor. I went for a piss and was washing my hands when I got dragged away from the sink by the back of my collar, I span round and was about to whack somebody... two blokes there, one of whom thrust a shiny badge in my face. Plain clothes CID (the scourge of funsters everywhere). 'We're searching you for drugs.' 'I haven't got any,' I protested. 'Empty your pockets.' 'You empty yours.' Slam. I went into the wall. 'Don't get fucking lippy.' 'OK,' I said as I emptied my pockets. (It was a tough call, a night in West Bar or a night getting wrecked in The Limit, mmm.)

"Anyway I emptied my pockets and got patted down, my change was on the sink (I had about £4 - hence no fags). I was wearing black German army combats – standard issue for us anarcho punks! The copper's face lit up as he pulled out a piece of folded crumpled A4 paper from my side pocket. 'What's this then?' 'A song.' He unravelled the paper and on it was written my latest lyrics for a song that the band had been practising – an anti police/system rant, I can remember thinking 'oh shit'.

"The copper took his time, read it and said 'it's not bad, that' before folding it up and putting it back in my pocket. 'If we catch you with any dope, we'll come down on you like a ton of bricks, now fuck off.' I couldn't believe it, I didn't even smoke dope, they must have watched me take that roll-up from that lad and 2+2=5! I never ever went out without any fags again, ever.

"Another time on a Thursday night, I can remember Lamby (Al) asking the DJ to play a request and the DJ wouldn't play it. The next thing I saw Lamby legging it out of the door and up the stairs and the DJ having a fit. The next thing, about three bouncers are running up the stairs. I'm thinking 'oh fuck, what's he done?'.

"All the punks, goths and psychobillys would look out for each other for the most part. Sheffield village. You could go out with £2 to your name and end up having one of the best nights ever."

Limit punters next to small bar Paul Unwin collection

"I end up chasing after the bouncers who are chasing after Lamby, we get to the top of Fargate and he's been nabbed by the old bill and there's three bouncers chomping at the bit. The DJ wouldn't play Lamby's request so he had wrenched the microphone off him and took to his heels. It was only about 11-o'clock. I can remember getting the thumbs up off Lamby, so off I tootled back to The Limit.

"Shirley (Chris Mclernon) pound-for-pound was the best chat-up artist I have ever met. There would be a really gorgeous girl arrive in the club with her boyfriend and Shirley had the capability to charm her away from him. Shirley had a line for any occasion and could talk a woman into any cubicle going. He once crawled on all fours towards a girl who was sat on the edge of the stage (she was wearing a mini-skirt) and started licking her legs, this was how he introduced himself; sat next to her was her boyfriend – Shirley, fearless!!

"Hooley had a habit of getting off with a barmaid, or at least befriending one, so that he could smuggle all the dregs from behind the bar so he didn't have to buy any pints. RIP dude.

"I can remember telling Big John (John Harrison) aka Sheffield Punk no.2 that this girl fancied him and was giving him the eye. John, bless him, used to have a bit of a stutter so chatting up the girls didn't always come easy to him.

"Anyway, John tootled over and within about five minutes they were playing tonsil tennis and John came back over to where we were standing near the bogs looking well pleased with himself. 'I-I-I-I've gggg-got her nnnumber.' 'John, it's a bloke'. 'Wwwhat?' 'She's a man.Y-y-you f-f-fuckin bbbastards.'

"The Limit for me in my formative teenage years was everything. I met so many quality people in that place who are still good friends to this day.

"Sometimes you would go in and there would be a right edge to the night. You would get scuffles to full-blown mini riots taking place.

"All the punks, goths and psychobillys would look out for each other for the most part. Sheffield Village.

"You could go out with £2 to your name and end up having one of the best nights ever.

"Football hooligans, gang culture, you can keep it. Limit RIP oh the memories."

"There was such a variety of music, something for everyone. I don't think a night went by without Grandmaster Flash's White Lines or a Nina Simone song being played amongst all this other mad stuff.

"There was no other club like it. I loved it at the time but it isn't until you look back that you can really appreciate the mad nights and mad people you shared your life with in The Limit. It changed for me in the late '80s, the Acid House thing happened and The Limit started catering for a different audience. I didn't care for it.

"The Limit was an alternative to all the other crappy clubs. The people were an alternative to all the other crappy people who frequented town. Then it started to cater for those crappy people and whatever spirit was left was lost. Football hooligans, gang culture, you can keep it. Limit RIP oh the memories."

'Sleeper in cubicle four' and the joy of 50p drinks

Former Limit barman Pip said: "Very occasionally we'd find someone asleep in the toilets after the club had shut. We'd shout 'we've got a sleeper in cubicle four' which would be the signal for a bouncer to pour a bucket of water over them – they'd come out looking very dazed.'

"We weren't allowed to use the tills to add up so had to do everything our in heads. We all loved 50p drinks night on a Thursday because it was easy to add up and we could all get pissed whilst we were working."

Punky Limit-goers take time out to skate in 1987, including the author, (second from right)

Punters on their way into The Limit Paul Unwin collection

Limit regulars from Paul Unwin collection

70 West Street, Sheffield 1 ☏ 730940
LIMIT CLUB
Every Monday Night
Latest USA & UK Dance Music
MUSIC BY D.J. ANT
Free Admission with this Ticket before 11.00 p.m.
(Except Bank Holidays)
P.S. Cheap Drinks : 11.30 to 12.30

LIMIT Club West Street
Mondays
It's the New Style !
D J - ANT
11.30 pm—12.30 am "CHEAP" Drinks Hour
FREE ADMISSION with this ticket

CLUB BOUNCER CLEARED OF BEATING REVELLER

NIGHTCLUB bouncer Michael Quirke was today cleared of claims that he beat up a reveller.

It took a jury at Sheffield Crown Court just ten minutes to return a not guilty verdict in the case.

It had been alleged that Mr Quirke assaulted David Turner at The Limit nightclub, in West Street, Sheffield.

He sustained a fracture to the back of his skull, a broken hand and severe bruising to his face and cuts, said prosecutor Morris Greene.

By Bill Brotherton

But Paul Watson, defending, said Mr Turner had an appalling criminal record and had been in prison and a young offenders' institution for violent offences.

Quirke, 43, a self-employed builder, married with two children, of the Old Vicarage, Eccles Street, Wincobank, denied inflicting actual bodily harm.

He said he had been a doorman for 22 years and had no previous convictions of any sort, whereas Mr Turner was a known trouble-maker.

On this night he was pointed out by a man who said he had hit him but had run into the foyer when approached, said Quirke. Once there he was attacked by the man's other friends and hit several times.

He tried to break it up but Mr Turner kept lashing out and he was forced to punch him about four times to defend himself.

"Most people that went to The Limit knew it was a rough place. There were people that took drugs and various other things. The group Mr Turner was with often caused trouble," said Quirke.

He had now stopped being a doorman following an incident in which he was attacked by 11 people and suffered injuries for which he need to to undergo a brain scan.

Mr Turner, of Cawthorne Close, Woodseats, said his friends were had been

CHAPTER NINE

Fractious relationships

AND UNWELCOME GUESTS

Limit owners George Webster and Kevan Johnson had totally different outlooks on life.Webster was the music-loving DJ and former record shop owner, Johnson was the ex-copper who knew the licensing trade because his dad operated successful pubs in the city.

There would never have been a Limit without them both.

Johnson had the business acumen, a ruthless streak and friends in the force and licensing trade: Webster had the club following, knew the music trends and had the contacts in the music industry.

Together they found exactly the right venue, the right staff (well they didn't quite find them, they simply nicked most of Wapentake Bar staff if truth be told with half of them splitting their time between both venues for the first few weeks of The Limit's life) and they hit on the right niche in the market.

Rifts were evident, according to key members of staff, in the Johnson/Webster relationship even before the venue opened but its immediate success, ability to make vast amounts of money and the availability of under-managers to act as go-betweens and mouthpieces when the two directors weren't talking ensured things moved steadily forward.

But it's not as if they were some unholy alliance that just got together to make The Limit happen and make a financial killing: they actually went back a long way, according to George Webster.

Paul Unwin said the rot set in virtually the day the club opened.

"George bought an RS Cortina in bright orange and a TR7 for his wife and that offended Kevan straight away. He was still travelling round in a battered old Audi. It was a total heap, you used to wipe your feet when you got out of it."

Fighting fire with raging inferno was soon the order of the day.

"Kevan thought 'well, if he's doing that, then I'm going to do the same' and he got a Nissan 260Z."

Martin Bellamy thought the start of the problems – often the case in Sheffield – actually all boiled down to football but for once didn't involve the reds or the blues of Steel City.

"He was still travelling round in a battered old Audi. It was a total heap, you used to wipe your feet when you got out of it."

The Limit opened just in time for the Argentinian World Cup of 1978 and Webster's pride and joy was a football fully signed by the victorious nation which used to take pride of place in The Limit office. Martin said: "Kevan got the ball out one night and decided it would be a good idea to have a kick about with the staff, so everyone joined in and we had a game of 5-a-side in the club.

"When it finished there was the realisation that all the autographs had rubbed off the ball. It was George's pride and joy – he must have gone mental."

Whether it was cars, football or a bit of both, the stage was now set for years of one-upmanship that would put even the most out-of-control rock stars to shame.

Paul Unwin: "George went out and bought this 32 feet long motor home complete with double bedroom, so Kevan bought a massive house on Long Line, Sheffield's self-titled millionaire's row.

"George went out and bought a massive house in Stocksbridge, complete with tennis court."

Though the spats between the pair (when they were actually talking, of course) became the stuff of folklore they were hardly that unusual in business.

There are few companies out there which don't have some match or other made in hell as the cornerstone of success: all-conquering operations are not built with yes-men at the helm.

The Limit was a very high profile and successful club, landing some of the biggest chart acts of the day: the list of hangers-on eager to strike up a friendship with George and Kevan would have been endless and the readiness of alcohol a non-stop temptation.

You need different ideas to keep things fresh and you're never going to get that with two people who sing from the same hymn-sheet all the time. But the relationship probably wasn't helped by the business Webster and Johnson were in.

The Limit was a very high profile and successful club, landing some of the biggest chart acts of the day: the list of hangers-on eager to strike up a friendship with George and Kevan would have been endless and the readiness of alcohol a non-stop temptation. They also hung out in totally different environments with completely different people.

George Webster was far more at home at a live gig, Kevan Johnson would crack open bottles of champagne at the glitzy Josephines nightclub nearby.

Throw in affairs, expensive divorces, lawsuits and you've got a recipe for total Armageddon, which was as good a word as any to describe the Webster/Johnson relationship by the end of the business.

One thing everyone seems in agreement with (the amount of cash generated definitely makes this argument stand up) is that The Limit was a very tightly managed operation, even when the ownership wasn't quite so tightly managed itself.

It employed the best legal and financial advice going.

Landing a job in senior management at The Limit must have been a dream come true.

You were paid up to quadruple the wage of any equivalent job in the city, according to Paul Unwin.

He said: "I was 23 years old and running about in an Indianapolis Pace Car on company petrol!"

But my the mid-eighties the fun had definitely gone out of things.

Paul Unwin: "Nobody was getting on with anybody and the club just became a means to an end. Everybody hated everyone else. If the club was quiet it was my fault.

"If people fought in the club it was my fault for playing the wrong music. If the stock was wrong it was Steve's [Bolderson] fault."

Tsunami time at 70-82 West Street

The combination of a bitterly cold winter and a long-forgotten water tank was behind an unexpected makeover forced on The Limit within months of its opening.

The incident was so unexpected it caused real fears that the fledgling venue might be finished.

Paul Unwin said: "We used to come in every morning at 9am. On this particular morning I opened the door from West Street as usual and as I was walking down the stairs I could hear water running. It sounded as though someone had left a tap on.

"I opened the door to the club and all I could see was water coming through the ceiling. What none of us knew was on the top floor of the factory building we were in stood a water tank that held over 3,000 gallons. This tank had frozen solid and then burst.

"The club was closed for a week before we'd even had a visit from the insurance company. During that time we had put the heating on to try to dry the place out and that had warped the wood on the dance floor."

The flood caused so much damage that The Limit ended up having a whole new makeover courtesy of the insurance cover.

Paul Unwin: "In a way it was a godsend but at the time we were seriously worried that the club might have to close as the damage was that serious. We were shut for around six weeks. We ended up with new lighting, new concrete floors, toilets re-done and we moved the stage from being opposite the main bar to being at the far end of the club, where it stayed until it shut. I think the last act to play prior to the flood were either Ultravox or The Members."

People were wowed with their shiny new Limit by all accounts. One re-opening night later, they were back in full swing.

Early morning Excise

The flood was nothing compared to the far more worrying and unexpected posse of visitors - a small army of Customs and Excise investigators.

This time The Limit managers weren't sure they were going to recover.

You have to hand it to the owners at this point: the venue's ability to make money and the amount it appeared to be actually making, virtually from day one, was mindboggling.

To put it in context: your average after-dark venue is lucky to have two good nights (Friday and Saturday) in a week.The Limit was doing six, plus the regular extra matinee shows, as well as hiring the likes of Sheffield City Hall and the Top Rank to promote larger gigs. That's before you even got to the bar takings.

Paul Unwin: "Everything made money, even the 10p coats made money and we were doing 500 of those a week. We could sell 10 barrels of beer in a week [with 36 gallons in a barrel that's just short of 3,000 pints a week] and that's before you even start on bottles and spirits."

Even a loose totting up of figures brings you rapidly to the conclusion that Limit-goers were either alcoholic multi-millionaires or there were 'issues' with the adding-up ability of the people on the door.

The flood was nothing compared to the far more worrying and unexpected posse of visitors - a small army of Customs and Excise investigators.

And there were probably far (and we mean far) more people in the club on many nights than should have been.

Figures of 1,200-plus for The Specials and Madness were offered many times.

So where did the admission cash from those alledged 880-plus punters over-and-above the licence regulated numbers go on those and any other nights?

Well, Customs and Excise had pretty rock solid conclusions as they´d had every member of Limit senior management under round-the-clock surveillance for weeks.

The Limit were actually very unlucky: apparently they had not started out as the people under investigation, that honour evidently went to the little mesters workshop adjacent, according to Paul Unwin.

He said: "Next door to The Limit was a chip shop with an archway and at the back of there was a little mesters workshop. Unbeknown to us, they were allegedly bringing in bags of half-crowns and melting them down for their silver content.

"Across the road there was an office furniture shop. Customs and Excise were holed up in an empty office upstairs watching the little mesters. But they were also armed with a clicker and one day they decided to start keeping a record of the amount of people going in and out of The Limit."

The huge volume of information they amassed gives an indication of the amount of time they'd spent on the case and how seriously they took the alleged goings on at The Limit.

It was early one morning when things kicked off. Paul Unwin was on holiday at his home in Sheffield when there was a loud knock at the door.

"I opened the door and there was this huge bloke standing there in a shirt and tie. He said: 'Mr Unwin?' And I said 'yes'. He said: 'I'm from Customs and Excise, have you got a minute?'"

Paul Unwin was arrested within seconds of opening the door. The Customs and Excise officer read him his rights and ordered him to report to The Limit for 10am the same morning.

What Unwin didn't know was that there were repeat performances happening to all Limit management across Sheffield.

"I immediately phoned George Webster and there was no answer. There was no answer from Kevan Johnson either. I couldn´t get hold of the accountants. I couldn´t get hold of anyone."

He couldn't quite believe what he saw when he arrived at The Limit that morning.

"There were Customs & Excise officials running about everywhere, the place was being turned upside down. They were emptying everything, from filing cabinets to cash registers. There was even one guy going through the bins outside."

The rest of The Limit management were already in the building.

"Kevan Johnson was sat in one corner of the room, George Webster in another and Steve Bolderson in another."

The magnitude of the situation quickly began to dawn on them.

"This guy came up to me and said: 'Now then, Mr Unwin, you don´t know why you´re here so I´m going to ask you a few questions.' The first question was: 'Do you handle monies for The Limit nightclub as part of your job?' I said 'no' and that I was a DJ and did promotions. He then repeated the question again."

Paul Unwin soon realised that Customs and Excise had been following his every move. The officer said: "I was stood at the side of you last week when you were paying monies in at Barclays Bank on West Street. Would you like to change your story?"

"They knew absolutely everything about me," confirmed Paul Unwin.

"They asked me how I could afford an Indianapolis Pace Car at 23 years old.

"They searched every inch of Kevan Johnson's house. They took the false roof down in his kitchen."

The amount of 'missing' money they were looking to account for was pretty staggering.

Paul Unwin: "They were looking for a quarter of a million pounds in unpaid VAT."

Certain faces were looking at the very real possible prospects of jail: the cost of the surveillance operation must have run into thousands of pounds.

In the end they agreed, according to Paul Unwin, on a figure of £60,000 and that was paid to Customs and Excise.

Despite the nightmare of the investigation, The Limit was still a dream account for any brewery.

"Kevan Johnson called Whitbread and said: 'Do you want The Limit's business?'. They said 'yes, yes' and he said 'how much is it worth?' and they said '£350,000'.

"So we took that off Whitbread, paid the VAT and we were back in business."

CHAPTER TEN

Last night of The Limit

THE DOORS **CLOSE** FOR THE LAST TIME

The last night at The Limit was arguably as legendary as its inception.

Answering 'yes' to the question 'did you go to the last night of The Limit?' is still capable of providing as much instant credibility as you'll ever need in many quarters of northern England.

Unfortunately, unlike at the opening night 13 years earlier which boasted little in the way of photographic evidence, your days are numbered if you claimed to have been there and are actually lying through your teeth.

Management filmed every second of the event and there are plans to do a DVD release in its entirety in 2011, the twentieth anniversary of the closure.

At the time, even if rumours had been flying around for months that the venue was soon to shut, people couldn't quite believe the end was indeed nigh.

Sheffield Hallam University student Chris Twiby was devastated.

"Tales about The Limit club was one of the main reasons I opted to do my degree in Sheffield. The venue was a legend in the North of England and many of my friends from Teeside used to make regular trips down there.

"I couldn't believe it was shutting within months of me moving into the halls of residence in Totley. Yeah, I'd read stuff in the papers about its threatened closure but you never think something with such an amazing legacy would really be allowed to go."

The West Street which the club said goodbye to on Saturday, January 19, 1991, was a very different animal to the one it had greeted in 1978.

There's no doubt The Limit had influenced and in many cases was still heavily influencing the night culture but the rebellion-charged punks and new wave aficionados had been replaced by the baggy movement and the rising dance revolution.

The last night was an instant sell-out and owner George Webster together with manager Gary Wilson greeted all guests personally as they entered the club for the last time. (They might be losing their club but all was not lost for The Limit team: Webster had already purchased The Palais venue on London Road, which was trading merrily.) Last-night punters were also treated to a two-hour free bar by Webster by way of thanks for their years of patronage.

As the management had nothing to lose that night, the event went on and on and on, way past normal closing time, by all accounts.

Usman Hasan, who was actually making his debut at The Limit, said:
"The event definitely had more the feeling of a celebration than a wake but obviously a two-hour free bar can help rescue some pretty dire situations.

"Everyone was in great spirits and there was such an amazing mix of people, from goths to rockers to dance kids."

And none of them wanted to go home that night.

Photos: Gary Wilson

Trinny Morris (middle) and George Webster (right)

John Quinn, journalist for Sheffield Star, said: "It may have been a funeral but the atmosphere was more akin to some sort of celebration.

"After 13 years, during which it provided a welcome alternative to the sanitised seductiveness of most other nightspots, The Limit Club on West Street finally closed.

"But there were no tears, at least not inside the venue, packed to the rafters with people for whom it had been part of growing up.

"No-one seemed perturbed by the £10 entrance fee – but then the drinks were on the management for two hours.

"Even after that, the crowd continued to increase and at one point the dance floor was so crowded that the disc-jockey had difficulty cueing up a record because the mass-movement caused the needle to jump.

"The type of people the club attracted due to its wear-what-you-want policy ranged from punks to hippies and from goth girls to beer boys, and the normally dressed-on-a-night-out brigade.

"But they were intent on having a good time, and the musical policy certainly helped them on their way.

"As some people were heard remarking, it was certainly the end of an era but the club's reputation for being the best place to hear music which is popular but considered too energetic to get played anywhere else remained intact until the very end.

Gary Wilson and clubber

Photos: Gary Wilson

"Now all that remains is a dingy building about to be boarded up and used for redevelopment and leaving a hole in the city's night scene which will probably never be plugged properly."

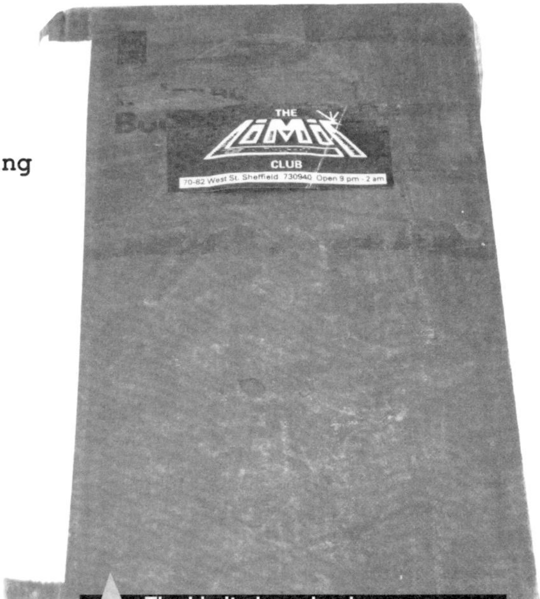

The Limit phone book

"The promise of favourite tracks dating back to the club's opening in 1978 was fulfilled, with the likes of The Stranglers, The Skids and some ska bringing the memories flooding back.

"And the dance floor was brought up to date with a selection of some more rhythmic hits of recent years.

"At the end, owner George Webster, a former dj who is now in charge of The Palais on London Road, stood on the stairs at the entrance, shaking hands with regulars, many of whom thanked him and wished him luck for the future.

"Now all that remains is a dingy building about to be boarded up and used for redevelopment and leaving a hole in the city's night scene which will probably never be plugged properly."

One thing which was absent on that last night was the venue providing the stage for a live band, the main reason it had opened up in the first place. That event had already taken place.

John Quinn said: "The Limit on West Street, once described as the most aptly named club in Britain, attempts to go out in style this week, with its final live concert before being bulldozed and converted into a car park.

"In its dozen years, it provided a starting point for many local bands and also featured concerts by many who were later to make it big, including our very own Def Leppard and Human League.

"On some occasions it provided the best night out in the city and on others it resembled the Black Hole of Calcutta with beer I wouldn't have wished on my worst enemy.

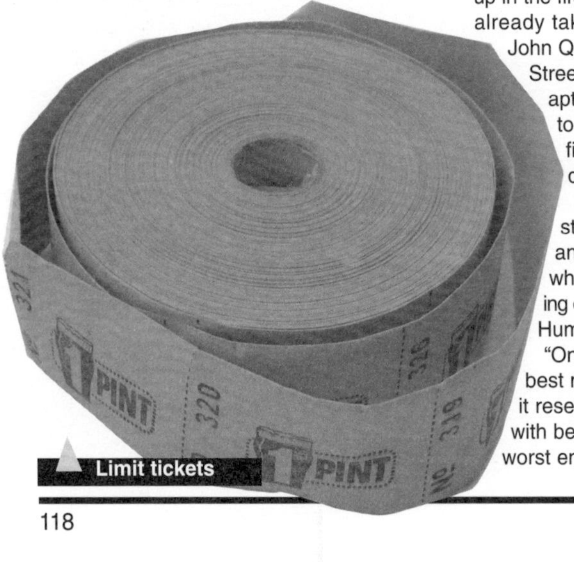

Limit tickets

"But soon, for all its faults and the fun it provided, it will be gone forever, with another couple of local acts helping us say goodbye.

"Headlining are The Lonely Hearts, who, for a change, don't appear to have changed their name for at least a week.

"And supporting them are Echo Park, whose main members, singer Steven Lay and drummer Anthony Beever, despite only being aged 19, actually played at the same venue almost three years ago."

"On some occasions it provided the best night out in the city and on others it resembled the Black Hole of Calcutta with beer I wouldn't have wished on my worst enemy."

The Limit lock and keys

Anything that wasn't nailed down on the closing night became a must-have item of memorabilia at the last night – chairs and tables were some of the most popular items making their way up the stairs and into the morning some time after 2am.

Limit manager Gary Wilson took everything from the red phone used to book the bands to the padlock and keys that secured the front door when the end of the lease closed the venue.

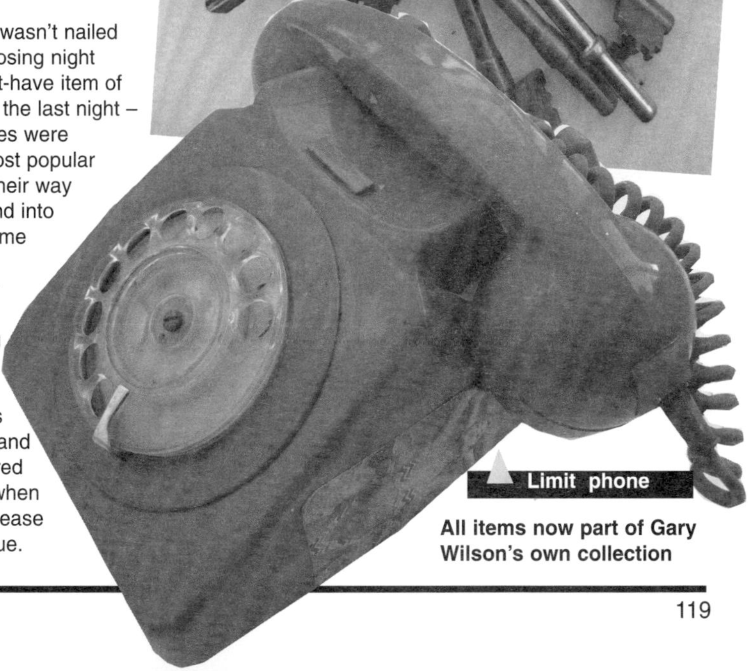

Limit phone

All items now part of Gary Wilson's own collection

Souvenir hunter, Palais barman and all-round aspiring Limit aficionado Hugh Ruiz said: "I had been working for George Webster as a barman at the Palais on London Road and had been chatting to some of the security staff there about George and the new gym he'd had built in his attic at his mansion somewhere in Sheffield when the news came through that the Limit was closing.

"Obviously living in Sheffield and being a young thing, for me The Limit was the place to go for it's distinctive music, décor and tables full of cheap pints.

"We had to get to the last night to see what souvenirs could be collected.

"Well it was closing down to be demolished and I did work for the owner... what was his was surely mine, no?

"So off we went on the very, very last night it opened.

"The townies or trendies have moved up from the town centre onto our beloved West Street, once the preserve of punks, students, rockers and people who generally wanted a great night out with cool music and little trouble."

"It was a sad occasion but I remember the toilets overflowing nicely and the beer just flowing wonderfully and the stickiness of the place being up to its dirty standards,

"We danced, we smoked, we stared at the floor and then drank more...

"As we looked up at the stairs to ground level on our last exit I remembered that I'd had a mission to take a little piece of history with me.

"So as I was nearly out of the club I grabbed the smallest and by far easiest thing to hide under your jumper... a bar stool!

"It felt great in my hands. I had an original part of The Limit.

"Unfortunately for the stool, we were so full of the sadness of The Limit's closing that the stool didn't make it very far.

"In fact it didn't even make it into my home. We were so full of Stella that it remained in the back of the taxi home... or so the story goes!

"What a place, though. I hope the driver who picked us up realised he was left with a historical stool in the back of his cab and that somewhere today the stool lives on, loved and in a place of honour in a Sheffield home."

Richard Chatterton was sad to say he missed the chance to pay homage to the club that had been his home for so long.

"There were two events I always regretted missing at The Limit. The first was the Delta Five/Monochrome Set gig I had to miss because I was ill, and the second was the last night.

"My partner Joanne went and bought me a "Last Night" T-shirt, which sadly I once wore to paint the house and is no longer with us.

"She told me many old faces were there, including my friend Tim, now one-legged Tim, who then had been touring with Joe Strummer of the Clash. Other venues tried to replicate the essence of The Limit years later but none captured the atmosphere and edge of the venue in it's glory years. Sadly the nearby Saddle pub also disappeared as did other pubs such as the Forresters and the Mailcoach, which would serve as a drinking stop on a Limit night out.

"The townies or trendies have moved up from the town centre onto our beloved West Street, once the preserve of punks, students, rockers and people who generally wanted a great night out with cool music and little trouble.

"The Hallamshire is still there, albeit called 'Rise at the Hallamshire' - a pub which hosted many a great performance from the musical hopefuls who used to play upstairs. Indeed Pulp played their mid nineties come-back gig here before they conquered the world, and after the so-called Brtit pop period there would be a re-awakening of interest in live performance which continues to this day and Sheffield is awash with places where local bands - folk, indie, goth, rock, jazz etc - can get up and play.

"And one of these, the Casbah, carried on the spirit of The Limit (and the rock club the Wapentake, on which the venue stood) for a few years.

"So here's to The Limit, the bands, the music, the people, the romances, the fights, the tears, the sticky floor, the flooded toilets, the LPs played early doors in their entirety - but most of all the fun,. I don't think I would have been the same person without it."

"So here's to The Limit, the bands, the music, the people, the romances, the fights, the tears, the sticky floor, the flooded toilets, the LPs played early doors in their entirety - but most of all the fun. I don't think I would have been the same person without it."

22 TELEGRAPH ARTS Sheffield Telegraph, Friday, January 18, 1991

The party's finally over at the Limit

Above: George Webster surveys his son-to-be-empty club. Right: George at the opening of the Limit in 1978

IT'S the end of the road for the club that once boasted Joy Division, Orchestral Manoeuvres in the Dark, Teardrop Explodes and Echo and the Bunnymen — on the same bill for just a quid.

After 13 years The Limit in West Street is closing down tomorrow night after a number of false alarms over the past year and attempts by owner George Webster to keep it going.

But now the party's over and tomorrow night will be the last chance to find out what all the fuss was about. The farewell bash will include free drink until 10pm (but will set you back £10) and also offer the last chance to hear the music that was the Limit's staple fare from 1978 onwards.

In its heyday the club boasted regular line-ups of names that would go on to become huge stars — bands like U2, Simple Minds, The Police, The Pretenders, The Buzzcocks, the list goes on and on. Sheffield's own superstars Def Leppard and The Human League also started off in the cavernous gloom downstairs at The Limit.

As well as the big names, The Limit was an important launch pad for local bands who have always struggled to find venues to play in the city.

In later years it became known as a regular student haunt and the big name acts dwindled. "Everyone who goes to The Leadmill has The Limit to thank — they got the idea from this place," said George Webster, reflecting on the past inside the club which is pretty cold and grotty in the chill light of day.

"When the Leadmill opened, Sheffield wasn't big enough for the both of us. But we were doing what the Leadmill does years before them."

George has particularly fond memories of Paul Young, who he describes as a great pal, who, with the Q-Tips, regularly packed the place out. And the times The Specials played and took their encore with dozens of fans prancing around the stage. And The Alarm, and Madness, and Annie Lennox and Ultravox . . .

The club has been under threat since October 1989, when the lease from the Manchester-based Co-operative Wholesale Society Property Group ran out. Others tenants in the building, including the snooker centre, have already moved out, but George hung on until the bitter end.

He got planning permission a couple of years ago to expand and develop The Limit from the basement to the ground floor, converting the current club area into a restaurant, but the Co-op decided to sell the property and the plan fell through.

George meanwhile has other irons in the fire. He owns the re-vamped Palais in London Road (formerly the Locarno) which featured on TV's Reportage last week. And he hopes to open his new club/bar/diner called Earl Street and Ellington's in Earl Street which will have a "jazz feel" in the city centre in the summer. He also has unspecified plans for another venue which should help showcase local bands.

But there'll be no more Limit Club after the weekend. The building will be demolished to make way for office space, although George jokes it will probably end up as an unofficial venue for acid house parties in the interim.

"I virtually lived here for ten years, and a lot of people in Sheffield have grown up with this club," said George. "It's the end of an era."

Jane Tadman

SHEFFIELD TELEGRAPH

NUMBER SIXTY-EIGHT, Friday, January 18, 1991

Twenty-five pence

The party is over as the Limit club closes its doors on the good times 22

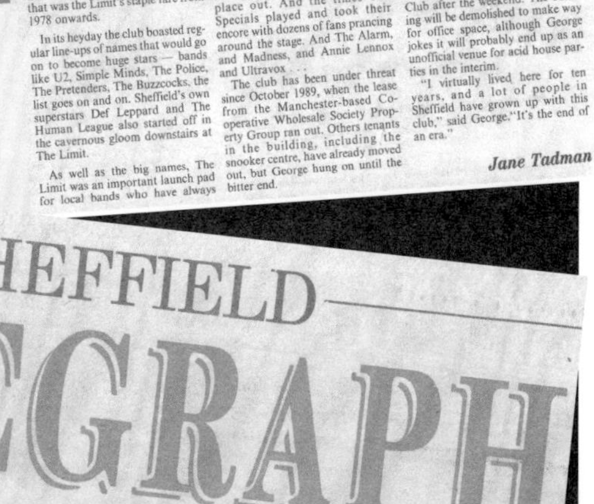

Articles in the Sheffield Telegraph about the closing of The Limit, January 18, 1991

opular Limit may go to make way for new car park

BULLDOZER THREAT TO NIGHTSPOT

By David Dunn

ONE OF Sheffield's most popular nightspots, The Limit, could be bulldozed to make way for a car park.

Sheffield Snooker Centre is also in jeopardy if the scheme goes ahead.

But widescale objections within the city centre are emerging, amid fears that the development could lead to a traffic nightmare.

More than 2,000 people have already put their names to a petition opposing the plans, which would engulf the entire club site and part of Trippet Lane.

The Co-operative Wholesale Society Property Group, which owns the site, has submitted an application to Sheffield Council to demolish the building and create a car park.

'UNBELIEVABLE'

Club owner George Webster is furious at the scheme, which kills off plans for extensive upgrading and expansion for The Limit.

He said: "The general feeling is that there is a policy to encourage cars into the city while most cities in this country are trying to discourage them.

"With a car park, you will have a situation with unbelievable amounts of traffic on roads that cannot handle the vehicles on them now."

Sheffield Snooker Centre owner Mike Watterson refused to comment.

The Co-op's Manchester office submitted the plans in June, but city councillors have yet to consider them.

3.11.89.

Baretta and passer-by
Photo: Chris Walker

CHAPTER ELEVEN

Life after the Limit

There's no doubt the end of The Limit was the end of an era for Sheffield nightlife but what exactly was that era?

The goths who frequented the popular Thursday alternative club nights of the mid-eighties probably had no idea that their heroine Siouxsie (of Banshees fame) was the first punk act to make a live debut in the place.

That was back in 1978, the stage was in a different place, Limit co-owner Kevan Johnson ended up having a huge argument with her after the show by all accounts.

He was out the picture by mid-eighties; he'd gone the same way as the six-nights-a-week music policy but he was the first one to click on to the fact that club nights were far more lucrative an option than paying musicians.

The rockers spent their lives down the Haymarket at Rebels in the mid-eighties only coming up town to visit the landlady of Wapentake Bar, Olga Marshall.
They'd never have known The Limit might have ended up as a rock club had she taken up George Webster's offer and become manager of his new club.

She hated punk and had already managed to persuade Trust House Forte to turn two of their flagship hotel bars into dark and dirty rock bars – George Webster and Kevan Johnson would probably have been a walkover.

There's no doubt the early years of The Limit were an absolute roller-coaster of a ride for the owners. The money going through the club was truly mindboggling. What would have happened if that Midas Touch feeling hadn't got the better of Kevan Johnson and George Webster and they'd left Sheffield Lyceum alone?

Would there be a Limit club in every UK city in 2009, as was once muted?

Would they still be on speaking terms? Questions, questions and not that many answers.

There's no doubt The Limit legacy – and it means many different things to many different people – is very real.

It was definitely a one-off, a venue that arrived in exactly the right place at the right time with the right formula.

My own experiences were of flooding toilets, sticky floors, great music (but also lots of crap) and some half-decent bands. When you look at the list in the cold light of day it's hardly a recipe for putting aside a few months to pen a book about the place and spend hours interviewing everyone you can find who had anything to do with it. Many say it's the seminal performances of bands from the early years or The Limit's staging of gigs by Sheffield bands that became the synth-revolution of the eighties that makes it so legendary.

"My own experiences were of flooding toilets, sticky floors, great music (but also lots of crap) and some half-decent bands."

But even that doesn't particularly stack up. Human League front man Phil Oakey didn't even like The Limit and local bands ended up hating the place.

The message boards of websites like Sheffield Forum and Sheffield History give an insight into why the ordinary punters loved it so much but common denominators like accusations of watered down lager and drinking warm cans of Red Stripe hardly make for a world-beating club.

Maybe it was simply The Limit's ability to fly in the face of the establishment that created the legend and brought together people who felt alienated by the mainstream clubs: it worked the same way for other Sheffield clubs of years before which had similar traits. Venues like Club 60/Esquire/ King Mojo and Black Cat.

George Webster and Kevan Johnson admitted taking inspiration from these early venues – they even employed Colin Duffield to do the majority of their own posters.The very same man who put together the artwork for Stringfellow's promotion of The Beatles at The Azena Ballroom in Gleadless - a poster that now changes hands for hundreds of pounds - and scores of other landmark gigs of that era.

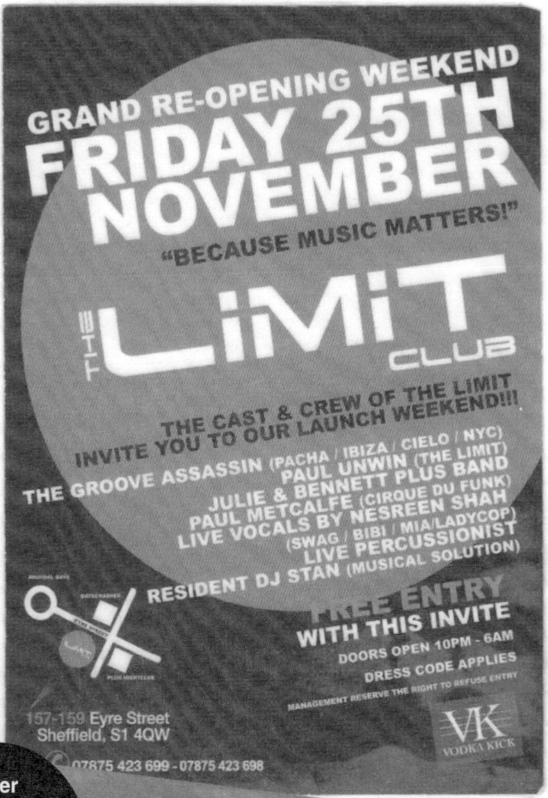

Flyer and pass from The Limit's brief reappearance in Eyre Street

So will their ever be another Limit?

Well there was – it just didn't last very long.

Original co-owner Kevan Johnston opened it on Eyre Street in 2005. It was a brave move and braver still that he didn't simply wind the clock back to 1978 (which would have probably signed its death knell ever quicker) when the first Limit opened.

Though he opted for some regular 'alternative' nights which saw Paul Unwin spin the discs made popular at the West Street predecessor, he opted to bring things bang up to date and open as a dance club. The nearest Sheffield actually got to a return to the spirit of The Limit – and brought many of the old faces together once again – were the halcyon years of The Casbah.

The lease of the bar which had been George Webster's stomping-ground decades earlier in its previous Wapentake incarnation was taken in part by former Limit-goer and ex-Def Leppard roadie Bob Mirfin.

His attempt to re-launch the venue as Wapentake Bar was losing money hand over fist so he took the brave decision (and the backlash from hell from the majority of Sheffield's rockers who, though they couldn't be arsed to drink there, soon came out of the woodwork to protest when there was a name-change in the offing) to re-name it The Casbah.

The name, which took its lead from The Clash's 'Rock The Casbah', was an attempt to open up the place to far more than a rock audience.

Armed with a 2am licence the place went bananas almost overnight.

There was hardly a person aged under 30 in there.

By 2000 it was drinking more lager than the majority of the Sheffield bars put together on a weekend.

It was full of ageing punks/rockers/indie kids/rockabillys and every other youth genre that ever set foot in The Limit seemed to have been reborn.

The music policy had more than a passing nod to Paul Unwin and his DJ friends from The Limit.

The former Club 60 also ran a Limit reunion night a couple of years later that saw Paul Unwin return to the decks and scores of old faces (including a few rather famous ones) crammed into the subterranean depths of West Bar.

It seems highly unlikely George Webster will be behind another Limit: he's now a tennis coach just outside London and has definitely "left the music business".

He seems very content and has no wish to return to running venues in Sheffield or anywhere else.

George Webster and Kevan Johnson made their fortunes at The Limit. They also lost them.

Kevan Johnson has bounced back more times than most.

He blames the failure of his 2005 Limit venture purely on location.

He makes no secret of the fact that he's keeping his eye out for any available properties on his old West Street stomping ground.

It's now nearly 19 years since the original Limit shut its doors for the last time and it's fair to say that, through the writing of this book, we've come to the conclusion that no one's really over it.

Precisely why we'll never know...

The Lord moves in mysterious ways - Limit posters in production in Colin Duffield's studio in the eighties

Richard Hawley played at The Limit in his early days with Treebound Story

Copyright Steve Stevlor

THE LIMIT

SHEFFIELD FORUM COMMENTS

ROUTE66
21-05-2008, 16:42
I went there from 1978ish to 1986. Went overseas then.
What a great place to have spent the 80s. Spent most of my time at the small bar drinking the German beer that was on tap (Holsten). The girl that worked behind the bar was Judy I think.
Wednesday night Students and Nurses I had the same free pass for many a year.
Happy times from what I can remember.
In those days you had to wear a tie to get in the other clubs in the town. The Limit was a free for all

THE LIMIT
1978-1991 R.I.P

tone78
20-05-2008, 18:47
A Francis Rossi lookalike who used to fly down the stairs attack a few punks, get 7 bells knocked out of him, cause a near riot, get slung out of the door by Egor then repeat the act the week after. Yes, happy days.
Take it to the Limit one more time...

lisalee
09-02-2008, 00:30
I remember the 'Hip Hop' afternoons held on Saturdays during the eighties! Wicked!!

I was waiting for someone to say that lol! I went Saturdays with my next door neighbour (Russell Gould), I was one of the very few laydee breakdancers lol!!! Ah, the good old days lol!!

morph
31-05-2007, 14:17
I remember the Student & Nurses night on a Wednesday at The Limit - 50p to get in and beer was free till 10.30pm (opened at 10pm) and they never blinked an eyelid at you coming up for 8 pints. Of course it was watered down, but I was only young and could get started nicely off the free stuff. And I remember lots of people skinning up in the shady seated area on the mid-right hand side.

datal
24-05-2007, 20:53
I remember seeing 'The Alarm' at The Limit. It wa so hot and sweaty that their spikey hair wilted.

As for Trevor 'Howcher' Jones, I

worked with him for many years. I believe he's now a very respectable (ahem!) member of the Foreign Office working at the British Consulate in Amsterdam. Top bloke!
Aaah Trevor, bless him, glad to hear he's doing well.

Grappler
27-04-2007, 19:22
I also remember the stage being located early on next to the DJ booth and remember seeing some great bands play there - Simple Minds, 999, Penetration. I also remember the Specials, Madness and Selector playing at the height of two-tone madness and The Limit was as packed that night as it has ever been. During my bar stint i also had the good fortune to see Aswad, Steel pulse, Black Uhuru, Sly and Robbie and a host of other magnificent reggae bands.

Some songs that always stayed with me from that time. Bingo masters break out - the fall The Puppet? Shack up - ACR, Emergency - 999GLC - Chelsea?
Chelsea Girl - Simple Minds New Rose -The DamnedTransmission - the great Joy Division

THE LIMIT 1978-1991 R.I.P

Englishmike
25-04-2007, 17:48
Anyone remember seeing Wham perform "young guns" at The Limit? they were so nervous that they didn't come out on stage the first time the song was played they stayed in the dressing room and only came out on the second playing and mimed the whole thing.

firesmudge
03-04-2007, 00:25
I remeber going to see the Cockney Rejects here in 70s there was a riot after the gig

Grappler
07-02-2007, 13:48
Aaah.... memories.
I worked at the Limit in the early days as a bouncer with Lew, when George Webster was managing him that sings "wherever I lay my hat" the band played there often & became famous.
Me & Lew were a friend of George we often went to his house at Grenoside,
I think he lived.

Suzie & the Bansheez, UB40, Bruce Springstine etc etc seen them all at The Limit.

I often used to get Trevor Howcher out of trouble at The Limit & the Leadmill, he used to 'like' me. (bless him)
I could tell you a few stories that would open your gobs in amazement but I can't on the SF. I later worked The Limit door with Gary Green, nice guy & clever, he ended up in Thailand & I think is a multi millionaire, I'm sure his fantastic pad was featured in one of those holiday progs.

I never did it, but the lads on the door often used to say to girls coming down the staires, 'show us your '****' & we'll let you in for nowt', some girls would willingly oblige & lift up their short skirts & give us a right eyeful, at the time it was funny, I cringe at the thought of it all now.

Later on Lew's brother Trinny worked there for years, one of the toughest guys I know, but this 'pipsqueak' for no apparent reason stabbed him in the stomach outside The Limit & ran off.

It was always too dark for me in The Limit & when any trouble broke out I could never see who the hell I was hitting.

THE LIMIT

1978-1991 R.I.P

algenon
21-11-2006, 06:38
what about when you went up West street first. in the Saddle(full of rockers), the West street hotel (Full of mods, students and with the table footy in), the Hallamshire (Full of goths and punks) and the Mailcoach.

What about all the crap on the bottom of your trousers from the loppy floor in The limit and if you ever fell over that was it you came out black.

Yes if you did miss the last bus it was a long walk home, twice as long if you were a bit wobbly.

DeanoGV
20-11-2006, 13:36
went to The Limit late 70s early 80s and saw some fab bands there Simple Minds,Specials and B-52s. Danced to punk, Goth, mod and electro in fact owt that they played.Does anyone remember dancing on the stage and always coming of with your nuckles bleeding as the roof was that low you always ended up punching it in the excitement.

The tables in front of the stage were always a good sliding point for some people to get off the stage.People falling asleep in the speakers. and always getting chips when you came out at the chippy next door. Some of the more individual people also used to go to the Sin Bin at turnups. Lots of happy memories.

You are " SPOT ON " !!!!
The Specials at The Limit was awesome much better than when they played the rank in the " two tone" concert. Happy days.

Do not forget walking on plastic glasses and getting your drinks from the small bar at the end near the entrance instead of queing up at the long bar.

Jabberwocky
09-07-2006, 12:13
I used to love the Limit in the mid to late 70s, I used to go in and get utterly bombed and quietly puke onto the floor, thats probably why it was so sticky.

It was the age of the punk so basically everybody puked and by 1.30 am we all looked like an ornamental fountain with the puke spurting and the coloured lights illuminating it to the sound of The Stranglers and Sex Pistols.

If I had a penny for every time I had to be carried, dead drunk up those stairs by a huge bouncer I'd...well I'd have 4p.

WhiteRabbit
30-08-2005, 23:28
What about the pie and chip shop next door to The Limit managed by a guy called Phil I think from Middlesborough?

I used to pop out all the time mid-way through the night for a quick pie and chips before going back in again, for some reason The Limit always gave me the munchies!!!

I remember several members of The Mission in there one night at the height of their 'fame' and one goth girl getting really friendly with Wayne Hussey.

About 4 years later I was coming round from anaesthetic in a Sheffield operating theatre's recovery room and she was the nurse stroking my head and asking if I was all right - totally bizarre!!

Idris
27-08-2005, 12:47
Originally posted by ceevee
Am I missing something?
I went once and once only around 89-90.

I stuck to the carpets. I saw big burly guys walking around taking money off little guys. You dare not look straight forward for fear of catching someone's eye, which invariably meant you were going to be stabbed. You looked straight up, or down at the carpet. The toilets were just used for rolling joints.

Wasn't The Limit one of the first clubs to introduce plastic cups?
Any reason for that? MMmmm.

Are you kidding? The tacky carpet and general dinginess were all part of what made it so great at The Limit...

THE LIMIT
1978-1991 R.I.P

I used to work there '88-89 as well - certainly was an experience...I have memories of working the Stella bar & having bottles chucked at me - maybe plastic cups were a good idea!!

gularscute
05-04-2005, 13:21
I remember rumours going round that the beer pipes were never cleaned in The Limit and that if you drank anything on draught you were guaranteed a bad head and guts. I've always wondered if that idea was floated by the management to get people to shell out on expensive bottled stuff.

The carpet was so filthy with generations of spilt drinks it seemed to be saturated in crude oil.

There used to be a big black guy who would periodically stride around chanting "Black hash, sensei, black hash" like a stoned street vendor.

Fantastic place, pity it can't be recreated as an antidote to the slick glamour places that have completely taken over where you get shot for looking at somebody funny.

FairyNormala
06-03-2004, 11:03
Limit was the first club I ever went to. I was 15 and went with my 14-year-old mate. Both mad goths, we looked years older than we were so got in easily.

I vaguely remember dancing on a stage, waving my arms around like a demented chicken!!! It was sooooooo cool going to school the next week and telling everyone we'd been to The Limit!

THE LIMIT
1978-1991 R.I.P

Originally posted by Spacehopper
8) Nah Den Ace........

Originally posted on Sheffield in the 80s............

I started going to the Limit regular from about '87. The music was an eclectic mix of punk/indie/goth/house. I used to drink lager snakebites in plastic glasses - a totally unique taste - it got you where you wanted to go though! I had a flat-top at the time.......anybody else remember the "Psychobilly" craze? I remember coming home with bruises all over my body from slam-dancing/ wrecking. Going to the toilet was a journey and an 'alf! First, you had to walk past the OCS (Wednesday boys), who used to congregate just outside the toilets. (To be fair, they never bothered any of us. I only ever saw them battling when United or the skin-heads came down!) There was always a dodgy black geezer selling drugs as you went in! The toilets were basically unisex - there would be couples copulating in the cubicles and there was a mirror in the lasses, so all the goths would go in there to do their hair!

I also remember sticking to the carpet, dry ice, the "Goth Box", anti-gravity hair and psychopathic bouncers - I too remember being thrown out the back door, a maze which led onto Trippet Lane!

The Hallamshire on West Street was my regular haunt and I also went to Take Two on Staniforth Road, "The Club With Two Brains" at Occasions, "Club With No Name" at The Palais, 50s night at The Dog and Partridge (on 'cliffe) and The Leadmill.

Great days! They broke my heart when they closed The Limit. I went on the closing night. When was that.......89/90/91?
I remember a bloke called John filmed it - has anybody seen it?
Regards,
Spacehopper.

Photo: Chris Walker

Matchbox at The Limit

Layout of The Limit

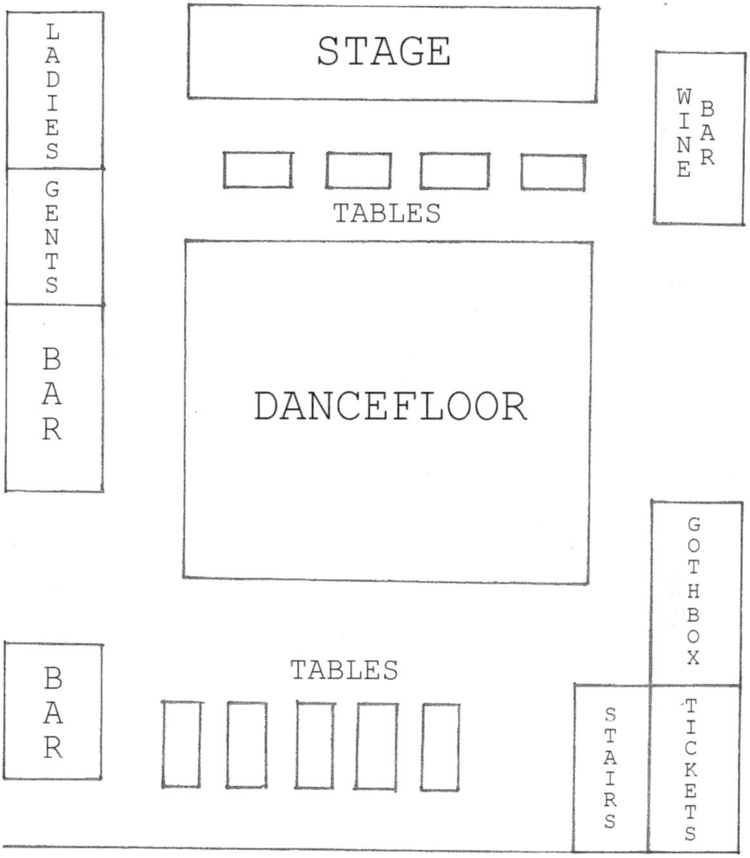

THE LIMIT

A list of the better known

A Certain Ratio
Adam and the Ants
After The Fire
Age of Chance
Altered Images
Angelic Upstarts
Artery
Aswad
Au Pairs
B-52s
Bad Manners
Barracudas
Bethnal
Big Wide World
Bill Nelson (ex Be Bop Deluxe)
Bitter Suite
Blue Rondo a la Turk
Boy on a Dolphin
Bram Tchaikovsky (Motors)
Cabaret Voltaire
Candy Paige
Chas and Dave
Chelsea
Cherry Vanilla
China Street
Chris Rea
Clock DVA
Cockney Rejects
Comsat Angels
DAF
Dalek I
Danse Society
Darts
David Johansen (including Sylvain Sylvain and Jerry Nolan of New York Dolls)
Dead Fingers Talk
Deaf Aids
Death Cult
Death Trash
Def Leppard
Defective Turtles
Delta 5
Department S
Depeche Mode
Disease
Dr and the Medics
Echo and the Bunnymen
Eddie & The Hotrods
Erasure
Eric Bell Band
Eurythmics
Fabulous Poodles
Fad Gadget
Fischer Z
Flamin' Groovies
Frank White
Freddy Fingers Lee
Funkapolitan
Gang Of Four
Gene Loves Jezabel
Generation X
Girlschool
Gloria Mundi
Gong
Guana Batz
Hula
Human League
I'm So Hollow
Joe Jackson
John Cooper Clarke
John Otway
Jools Holland/Millionaires
Joy Division
Killing Joke
Landscape
Lena Lovich
Level 42
Little Angels
Macc Lads
Madness
Magnum
Marillion
Matchbox
Matumbi
Merton Parkas
Mirror Crack'D
Modern English
Monochrome Set
Nash the Slash
Nine Below Zero
Orange Juice
Orchestral Manoeuvres In The Dark
Original Mirrors
Paul Bower (ex 2.3)
Penetration
Person to Person
Peter and the Test Tube Babies
Peter and the Wolves

THE LIMIT

bands that played

Pink Military
Ponders End
Psychedelic Furs
Pulp
Punishment of Luxury
Purple Hearts
Q-Tips
Rich Kids
Robert Cray
Roger Chapman
Roman Holiday
Secret Affair
Sharp Cuts
Simple Minds
Siouxsie and the Banshees
Skids
Slaughter and the Dogs
Sniff and the Tears
Soft Cell
Sonja Christina's Escape
Sons and Lovers
Sort Throat
Squeeze
Starjets
Steel Pulse
Steve Earle
Subway Sect
Swans
Teardrop Explodes
Terry & Jerry
The Adverts
The Alarm
The Associates
The Beat
The Berlin Blondes
The Blockheads
The Blues Band
The Bodysnatchers
The Chords
The Cramps
The Cure
The Dickies
The Durutti Column
The Eric Bell Band
The Extras
The Fabulous Poodles
The Headboys
The Honeydrippers (featuring Robert Plant)
The Inmates
The Jags
The Lambrettas
The Lurkers
The Mekons
The Members
The Men They Couldn't Hang
The Meteors
The Modettes
The Naughtiest Girl Was A Monitor
The Next Band
The Photos
The Planets
The Polecats
The Pretenders
The Push
The Rezillos
The Ruts
The Selecter
The Shamen
The Shirts
The Specials
The The
The Thompson Twins
The Tourists
The Undertones
Theatre of Hate
Tom Robinson
Tony Capstick
Toyah
Treebound Story (with Richard Hawley)
Tribesman
U2
UB40
UK Subs
Ultravox
Vice Versa
Violinski
Vision
Vitamin Z
Wall of Voodoo
Wasted Youth
Weapons Of Peace
Wham
Wilco Johnson
Wild Horses (with Brian Robertson and Jimmy Bain)
Wire
Wreckless Eric
999

DJ Paul Unwin's playlist from 1978

Artist	Track	Album
Patti Smith	Because the Night	Easter
Bruce Springsteen	Badlands	Darkness etc
Bruce Springsteen	Candy's Room	Darkness etc
Buzzcocks	Ever Fallen in Love	Love Bites
Buzzcocks	Love you More	Single release only
Rollng Stones	Hot Stuff	Black & Blue
The Only Ones	Another Girl Another Planet	The Only Ones
Talking Heads	Psycho Killer	Talking Heads 77
Wire	I Am The Fly	Chair's Missing
Ian Dury	Sex & Drugs & Rock & Roll	New Boots & Panties
Ian Dury	Clever Trevor	New Boots & Panties
Ian Dury	Wake Up And Make Love	New Boots & Panties
Dr Feelgood	Roxette	Stupidity
The Motors	Forget About You	Approved by the Motors
Devo	Mongoloid/Jocko Homo	Are We Not Men
Devo	I Can't get No Satisfaction	Are We Not Men
Magazine	Shot By Both Sides	Real Life
Generation X	Ready Steady Go	Generation X
Stranglers	Tank	Black & White
999	Emergency	999 Album
Ramones	Blitzkreig Bop	Ramones
Cheap Trick	I Want You To Want Me	Single release

Artist	Track	Album
Elvis Costello	Pump It Up/Chelsea	This Year's Model
Ultravox	Slow Motion/Quiet Men	Systems Of Romance
Rezillos	Top Of The Pops	Can't Stand The Rezillos
The Movies	The Last Train	Bullets Through The Barrier
Jonathon Richman	Egyptian Reggae	Single Release
Tom Robinson	Glad To Be Gay	Power In The Darkness
Reggae Regulars	Black Star Liner	12 inch version
Steel Pulse	Handsworth Revolution	Handsworth Revolution
Steel Pulse	Ku Klux Klan	Handsworth Revolution
Steel Pulse	Prodigal Sun	Handsworth Revolution
Japan	Adolescent Sex	Adolescent Sex
Siouxsie & The Banshees	Hong Kong Garden	Single release
Eddie & The Hot Rods	Do Anything You Wanna Do	Single release
X Ray Specs	Identity/ Germ Free etc	1978 singles
Gloria Mundi	Fight Back	I Individual
Public Image Ltd	Public Image	First Issue
Bob Marley	Easy Skanking	Kaya
Kraftwerk	Neon Lights	Man Machine
The Adverts	No Time To Be 21	Crossing The Red Sea
Richard Hell	Blank Generation	Blank Generation
Adam & The Ants	Deutcher Girls	Jubliee 1977
Blondie	Telephone/Denis/Heart of	Parallel Lines

The author

Sheffield-born Neil Anderson has written on music and entertainment for titles spanning The Independent to The Big Issue.

He was a Sheffield Telegraph columnist for over a decade and wrote the city's renowned Dirty Stop Out's Guide.

Neil started life as a hairdresser but saw the light when he landed a job in Sheffield City Hall's publicity office.

He unwittingly started researching this book in the mid-eighties as part of a mis-spent youth project that demanded regular attendance at The Limit.

When he's not writing books about long-gone dens of iniquity he's running a successful media relations agency (All Credit Media) or finding other excuses for not getting a proper job.

He also spent a few years as the regular Saturday night DJ at Sheffield's Casbah venue (formerly Wapentake) – the only venue to get anywhere near re-creating The Limit vibe in Sheffield.

Sub editing - Maggie Soutar   Research - Emma Greendale

Acknowledgements

Thanks to everyone that has helped me on a six month journey from fleeting idea to conclusion. In no particular order Martin Lilleker (and thanks for the okay to lift bits of your wonderful book), John Quinn, Dave Dunn, Gary Wilson, Steve Bolderson, Phil Oakey, Hugh Ruiz, Debbie and Mark Albrow, George Webster, Kevan Johnson, Joe Elliot, Rick Savage, Andy Smith, Lee Ford, Mark Hobson, Colin and Jason Duffield, Tony Beesley (and thanks for the okay to lift bits of another wonderful book), Peter McNerney, Brendan Moffet, Phil Staniland, Olga Marshall, Martin Bellamy, Paul Young, Bitter Suite, Janet Barker, Paul Unwin, Klive Humberstone, Clive Porter, Jon Downing, Colin Dixon, Damien Wilkinson, Pete Hill, Steve Stevlor, Tracy Pidd, Garry Bond, Richard Chatterton, Phil Wright, Jane Salt, William Coopland, Paul Davis, Geoff at www.sheffieldforum.co.uk, Steve at www.thewookie.com, Nigel Renshaw, Michael Farnell, Ivan Bradley, Bailey Brothers, Martyn Ware, Glenn Gregory, Deborah Egan, Chris Walker, Geoffrey Beattie, Pip Thorne, Barbara Fenton, Alison Leeming, Chris Peach, Peter Martin, Keith Strong, Ian Soutar, Pete McKee, Michael Glover, Stephen Bruce and Mary Slocombe, Glenn Ashley, Ian Cheetham, Sheffield Newspapers (thanks for the use of the fantastic photos), Karen Davies, Martin Lacey (and thanks for the okay to reproduce NMX fanzine) and Karl Lang.

Thanks to the following artists for getting me through this book and keeping me relatively sane: Iggy Pop, Killing Joke, The Ramones, Richard Hawley, Magazine, Billy Talent and Rancid.

Book design and layout: Ann Beedham

Further reading

(both books contain chapters on The Limit):

Martin Lilleker's 'Beats Working For A Living – Sheffield Popular Music 1973-1984'

Tony Beesley's 'Our Generation' (www.ourgenerationpunkandmod.co.uk)

www.sheffieldforum.co.uk

www.thewookie.com

www.sheffieldhistory.co.uk

Human League at The Limit by Pete McKee

Limit crowd Photo: Phil Wright

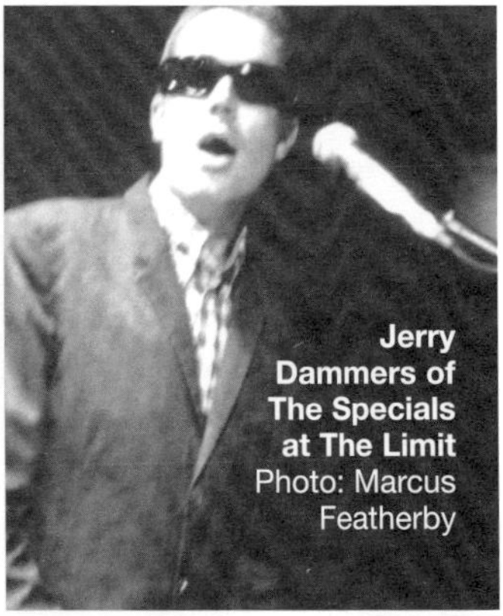

Jerry Dammers of The Specials at The Limit Photo: Marcus Featherby

Nigel Renshaw on stage with the Stunt Kites Photo: Nigel Renshaw collection

Photo: Michael Farnell collection

Phil Wright (middle) and friends after meeting Secret Affair Photo: Phil Wright

Limit glass collector Barry Photo: Phil Wright

Limit regular
Mike Chapman
Photo: Karl Lang

Limit regulars Dawn and Simon Photo: Karl Lang

Limit regulars Photo: Nigel Renshaw

Flexible Penguins at The Limit including Michael Farnell (sitting at front) and guest guitarist Steve Genn (middle, stood at back).
Photo: Michael Farnell's collection

THE REEL MONTY
Now with
SHEFFIELD INTERNATIONAL CITY
the follow up !
The Star
Creativesheffield.
City On The Move
35th anniversary edition
ACMRETRO